The Mirth Manifesto

Why merriment can breathe new life into the church

STEVE MORRIS

Copyright © 2022 Steve Morris

First published 2022 by Authentic Media Limited,
PO Box 6326, Bletchley, Milton Keynes, MK1 9GG.
authenticmedia.co.uk

The right of Steve Morris to be identified as the Author of this Work has been asserted in accordance with the
Copyright, Designs and Patents Act 1988.

All rights reserved.
No part of this publication may be reproduced, stored in a retrieval system, or transmitted in any form or by any means, electronic, mechanical, photocopying, recording or otherwise, without the prior permission of the publisher or a licence permitting restricted copying. In the UK such licences are issued by the Copyright Licensing Agency, 5th Floor, Shackleton House, 4 Battle Bridge Lane, London SE1 2HX.

British Library Cataloguing in Publication Data
A catalogue record for this book is available from the British Library.
ISBN: 978-1-78893-175-5
978-1-78893-176-2 (e-book)

Unless otherwise noted, Scripture quotations are taken from
The Holy Bible, New International Version Anglicised
Copyright © 1979, 1984, 2011 Biblica Used by permission of Hodder & Stoughton Ltd, an Hachette uk company.
All rights reserved.
'niv' is a registered trademark of Biblica
uk trademark number 1448790.

Scripture quotations noted nkjv are taken from the
New King James Version®. Copyright © 1982 by Thomas Nelson.
Used by permission. All rights reserved.

Scripture quotations noted (kjv) are taken from The Authorized (King James) Version. Rights in the Authorized Version in the United Kingdom are vested in the Crown. Reproduced by permission of the Crown's patentee, Cambridge University Press.

Cover design by Luke Porter
lukeporter.co.uk

To my dad, Ralph, who made me laugh.

CONTENTS

Foreword — vii

PART ONE: Setting Course
1. First Word — 2
2. The Quest Begins — 5
3. The Mirth and Merriment I Grew Up With — 26

PART TWO: The Theology of Mirth
4. The Comedy Slackers — 42
5. Creation Laughs — 49
6. Jesus and Humour — 58
7. The Incarnation — 69

PART THREE: Outbreaks of Mirth and Merriment
8. Politics, Fools and Speaking into Power — 82
9. Of Golf Courses and Helter-skelters — 95

10	The Unintentional Merriment and Mirth of Church	105
11	The Comedy Vicar	122
12	Stand-up and Be Counted	134
13	Bring on the Clowns	152
14	Foolish Saint: Martin Luther	163
15	The Holy Fool: St Francis	170

PART FOUR: The Renewed Church

16	Building the Merry and Mirthful Church	180
17	Signing Up to the Mirth Manifesto	198
	Last Word	211
	Notes	213

FOREWORD

Wonderful word, 'mirth', isn't it? It calls to mind, for me, hazy days as an undergraduate, laughing uncontrollably in pub gardens. I forget the substance of the jokes that induced such episodes, but the memory of the laughter, the mirth, remains. It is a broad and generous word – a syllable stretchable enough to include all sorts of remembered definitions of joy. You will have your own, no doubt, and I *do* hope you're smiling as you recall them now. It is, I think, a great feat to have the title of a book alone induce a smile. Steve Morris's skill in the text that follows this humble foreword is to keep that smile going, and to ensure, behind it, the brain and the heart are engaged as well.

How so? Well, firstly, this *Mirth Manifesto* is joy-giving. No dry Lenten course lies before you, dear reader. Though it is profound and thoroughly researched, it stands in that good and ancient tradition of presenting the holy and the true alongside anecdote and aside. Whether it is tackling stereotypes or showing us the saints, this is a tome that will instruct, but which I would wager you will also – shock and horror! – actually enjoy.

Secondly, this manifesto is confidence-giving. In Genesis 21:6, Sarah exclaims 'God hath made me to laugh, so that all that hear will laugh with me' (kjv). Laughter and joy are profoundly attractional and, as the church as a wider community of believers comes to difficult questions about how it might safeguard its future, a missiology of mirth – as is gently and wisely laid out here – will serve us very well indeed.

Finally this manifesto is a reminder that laughter is, and has always been, at the heart of the Christian faith. In her Scriptures, in her saints, and in her strange and holy people in churches around the world, there is much that sparks joy. A repropagation of that heritage is long overdue.

Indeed, it is much to be wished that this ancient appreciation of godly laughter might make a return. This joyous tract is a wonderful step in the direction of the restoration of such a mode of thinking and of laughing as well, for God and laughter are no strangers to one another. The *Risus Paschalis* is an ancient tradition of an eruption of laughter at Easter. It is not the mocking cackle of disbelief, but rather the spontaneous mirth of revelation. After all, what could be a better punchline than the defeat of death? The revelation that God really was on our side all along?

So embrace *The Mirth Manifesto*, my brothers and sisters. For at the heart of Christianity is the earthly echo of cosmic laughter and heavenly joy. After all, the joke is good – in the truest sense – and justifies not only our mirth but our whole fallen human race. If that sounds intriguing, then I would urge you to read on.

Revd Fergus Butler Gallie
London

I believe there is a great deal of false reverence about. There is too much solemnity and intensity in dealing with sacred matters; too much speaking in holy tones.

C.S. Lewis[1]

Shout for joy to the LORD, all the earth.
Worship the LORD with gladness;
come before him with joyful songs.

Psalm 100:1,2

PART ONE

Setting Course

1

First Word

Alan, an actor, had been out of work for months.[1] He was fed up, depressed – even the food cupboard was bare. In his desperation he turned up one morning at his local zoo, found the manager and asked if there were any jobs going. 'What do you do?' asked the manager. 'I'm an actor.' The manager's face lit up. 'I've got just the job for you,' he said. 'Our gorilla died in the night and he was one of the zoo's stars. Put on this gorilla suit and get into the cage.'

A rather nervous Alan, clad in gorilla suit, entered the cage. Initial stage fright was calmed by his professional experience and soon he enjoyed the laughter of people as he ate bananas, climbed branches and swung on the swings. The swings amused people most – which made Alan more and more adventurous. He got carried away, swung too high, went over the fence, and landed in the lions' enclosure.

And, yes, there was a large lion with big eyes staring at the invading gorilla. Alan was terrified, his knees knocked through his gorilla suit and, when the lion stood up and approached him, the sweat ran down his back. He gave up. He was paralysed. The lion slowly walked towards him and lifted his nose up to Alan's face. A long pause – and then Alan heard a voice: 'Don't panic, carry on acting, or we'll both get the sack.'

What is the real deal? What is the real thing?

Are we hiding, like the actors, behind a façade? Perhaps the truth is, mirth is much more important than we thought it was. Perhaps humour and mirth and all the good things are at the centre of the faith. So often we hide behind our knowledge and our theology and our teaching. But what if the best response to God, and

> The way of mirth is dangerous.

the best way to express it, was simply to be more carefree, silly and to decide to be merry? This book asks that: what if?

The way of mirth is dangerous. It might mean we have to sacrifice our dignity. We may have to give up some control. We may end up with the lions.

2

The Quest Begins

Before I became a Christian in my forties, I had a low opinion of church. In fact, I had barely been in a church since I was in my teens and had to go to church in order to get into the Scouts' football team. I associated church with being serious and feeling cold in winter and wanting to get home and get on with my life. I had a suspicion that Christians might lack a sense of humour – or at least a sense of self-irony.

As a boy, in church, I found many things funny that I shouldn't have. I wondered why everyone else didn't find some of the things we did a bit ridiculous.

The story of how and where I ended up in church in my forties and became a Christian is for elsewhere. But before that day, the one thing I know is that I did not associate mirth and merriment and humour with church. They seemed to come from a different realm. Like so many people, I had a vision of church as a place that was solemn. It was a place for hushed voices and Sunday-best behaviour.

I got my fill of mirth and merriment elsewhere. Comedy clubs, parties, good times with friends, fun at work with colleagues, they all played a great part in my life. They added light and shade. I was no rabble-rouser at all, but I loved life when it was full of fun and lightness. I like the joy of hearing something funny or saying something funny. I like a bit of slapstick and banter.

I have long wanted to go on a quest to see whether we need more mirth and merriment in church. I wondered if I had missed something or that we were, more generally, missing out on something. Should the faith and the church feel much more foolish, much more light-of-heart?

But then, I wonder what the God who so scrupulously outlined the nuts and bolts of putting together the temple in the Old Testament would make of the chaos and messiness of merriment? I worry about it. I struggle to get through those Old Testament books that deal with how to build a temple. I can't for the life of me see why God cared so much. Especially as when he came in person, he seems to be, to say the least, a little slipshod about the rules.

As a vicar, I think it is fair to say that I lead a messy church. I don't mind when there are mistakes. I revel in my congregation's eccentricities, and I sometimes find myself laughing during a service when something funny happens, much as I did as a teenager. I find church funny. That may be because I always find it hard to be forced to be serious. It may be that in church people don't really feel at their ease, and so sometimes they make a blunder.

A while ago a parishioner came up to me looking a bit panicked.

'What's up?' I asked.

'I can't do the reading today; I have to go home.'

I presumed that she was ill or a family member needed urgent medical assistance.

'That's fine,' I said. 'Can I pray?'

'No, it's OK,' she answered. 'I have to go and put my rice pudding in the oven.'

I have a great deal of hope that merriment and messiness and mirth are about to make a comeback. Perhaps it just needs a little encouragement and reassurance that the church won't fall down if we take ourselves less seriously.

The misplaced laugh

I worry about God and laughter. Right at the start of the Bible, in Genesis 18, a character called Sarah has the same thought. She has heard angelic visitors saying that she is going to become pregnant, despite being well past child-bearing age.

> So Sarah laughed to herself as she thought, 'After I am worn out and my lord is old, will I now have this pleasure?'
>
> Then the Lord said to Abraham, 'Why did Sarah laugh and say, 'Will I really have a child, now that I am old?' Is anything too hard for the Lord ? I will return to you at the appointed time next year, and Sarah will have a son.'
>
> Sarah was afraid, so she lied and said, 'I did not laugh.'
>
> But he said, 'Yes, you did laugh.'

It is one of those moments like when a teacher suddenly turns their attention to you when you've been giggling. I have to say, I find the passage chilling. Why shouldn't she laugh? I think I would laugh right now if some angels turned up and said that I was going to run the 100 metres in 6.4 seconds flat.

God seems to be standing on his dignity, which is a problem.

Meeting the Dalai Lama

Out of the blue, I'd received an invitation to go to St Paul's Cathedral to see the Dalai Lama receive the Templeton Prize. I suppose I wasn't sure what to expect. But his speech certainly was a turn-up. I remember him breaking out into giggles on a few occasions for no apparent reason. It was beautifully silly and met with a kind of amused reticence from those in attendance. I cannot remember all that he said. But I can still remember the giggles.

To put it mildly, I don't think that this was St Paul's usual style. He won the prize, more than a million dollars, which he said he would give to charity.

After the service, I managed to find a back entrance in the cathedral and get into the VIP reception in the crypt. I am still embarrassed about the first part of that bean-feast. Spotting a prominent member of the clergy, I decided to say a quick hello. It didn't help that I think I scared him by creeping up on him, but the minute I'd said hello, I realized I had absolutely nothing else to say and wanted to say an immediate goodbye.

After a horrible couple of minutes, we wandered off from each other, relieved that the pain was over. I felt awkward and clumsy and rather English.

It was then that I spotted the Dalai Lama walking down a line of dignitaries and smiling. In for a penny, in for a pound – I elbowed my way into the VIP line-up. As he got to me, his eyes lit up. He was smiling at me, I was sure. I wondered if he thought that he recognized me.

His pace slowed. And then, without warning, he touched me on my shoulder and put his hands in mine. What followed was a kind of hand-dance, with each of us moving our arms up and down like kids in a playground. Then he leaned in towards me and rubbed his forehead on my forehead. He hugged me to him.

It was so beautifully precious and childlike that I could have cried. His Holiness and I were in a bubble. It was as though a great dollop of joy and happiness had enveloped me.

THE QUEST BEGINS   11

That afternoon, I went to do a communion service at a local care home. I always slightly dreaded it – the plight of these magnificent old people would live with me for hours afterwards. It certainly wasn't a place of joy, that's for sure. I mentioned to one of the staff what had happened at the cathedral.

Moments later other staff members, all from Tibet, came to see me. They wanted to rub their foreheads on my forehead – my head was, apparently, full of a kind of deep holiness. And so, in front of a room full of people, many of whom had forgotten who they were, we re-enacted that odd moment of connection.

I was the man who had touched the Dalai Lama. I felt like not washing for a week.

A few years later, I read a book that helped me to make sense of what happened. That glorious double act Desmond Tutu and the Dalai Lama produced *The Book of Joy*.[1] It really is a joy and draws some sharp contrasts between a Buddhist and Christian way of looking at the world.

At one point the Dalai Lama explains that when he meets someone with real joy on their face, his own heart rises to a sense of joy as well.[2] He mirrors the joy and fun in another person and rubs foreheads with the individual concerned.

The individual on that day was me. The Dalai Lama passed down a huge line of dignitaries – the great and the good, bishops aplenty, archdeacons and the like. But it was just the curate he picked on to rub foreheads with and to create a bubble of merriment.

There is something deep about the Dalai Lama's approach. He makes sure to look for joy and mirth and, when he finds it, to pass it back and pass it on. We are all baton-carriers of mirth. We are all part of a relay team that, when it spots the joy of mirth and of life itself, decides not to keep them to ourselves.

Is mirth childish?

I used to think that being serious was grown-up and that mirth, merriment and humour were childish. St Paul talks about leaving the ways of childhood behind him (see 1 Cor. 13:11), which always seems a bit of a shame. There are times when I feel as though if I was more like a child, I might be a much better person to be around.

I worry that our institutions, including the church, think the same way. It was when an odd question presented itself to me that I began to wonder otherwise. What if mirth and humour and merriment were actually the real sign of being a grown-up?

THE QUEST BEGINS

Why are humour and mirth part of being a grown-up? Humour and mirth thrive on the absurdity of the human condition, and this takes a level of insight.

Perhaps a church that is too certain and unable to take itself and the faith and each other a little lightly is like the tree with shallow roots. Humour and mirth speak of a kind of freedom not to always see things as they are. They speak of a freedom to be silly and to jest in the face of tragedy and uncertainty. Indeed, they see these as a medicine. That's why I wanted to find out more about mirth and merriment and church.

> Humour and mirth thrive on the absurdity of the human condition.

Mirth and merriment . . . and humour

I certainly want to be clear about my terms, but mirth and merriment and all the associated words feel a bit slippery. It is as though as we are laughing, they take on something of a life of their own.

Let's begin with mirth. It has the feeling of an old word which is something that I like. You don't often hear the word actually used and are more likely to hear many of the synonyms: 'cheeriness' and 'cheerfulness', which immediately sound appealing. I like the idea of a cheery church and vicar and a cheerful God and saints and apostles and the like.

Mirth means being cheerful; it means laughing. It implies an aversion to earnestness. It encompasses one of the great forgotten verities – silliness. It also has associations with a certain abandonment – exhilaration, glee, pleasure and amusement. And then there's blitheness; a wonderful word that means to me doing things without being weighed down with anxiety.[3]

To be mirthful is to have the time to stop thinking for a while and to laugh. While in the grip of mirth, we might be less concerned with needing to answer every question or know the ins-and-outs of everything.

The word does indeed transport us back across the centuries – who could resist the notion of frolicsomeness? Although it sounds perhaps a bit ribald and dangerous. It is certainly at odds with the image many non-churchgoers have of church.

But what we get overall is the wonderful flexibility of a word like 'mirth'. And the picture one gets is of something that is very appealing, and the very opposite of a life that is closed-up, angry or dry.

THE QUEST BEGINS

Mirth looks rather like a way of looking at the world and being part of it, rather than just having a quick laugh. Mirth is something that we have within, and it is not just laughing all the time. Laughing all the time would be deeply dull, and perhaps even moronic.

And we need to make sure that we don't miss the edge to mirth. Mirth and humour can sometimes be both prophetic and dangerous.

Mirth is about taking and giving joy in our everyday life. Laughter is part of mirth. It is one of the engines of mirth but it isn't the car, to use a metaphor. Sometimes mirth might be expressed as a smile, or perhaps a giggle.

Merriment seems to me to be a simpler idea. To make merry is to actively have fun and to enjoy the company of others. To be merry is to laugh and sing and tell stories and even to dance. At least, that's the way I am defining it. Merriment doesn't need to be raucous, of course. It can be quiet and gentle and shared with a few. It can be a merry family gathering marked by good humour and cheer. It can be a church dinner. It can be a Bible study group that suddenly discovers a sense of humour and joy.

Both mirth and merriment suggest a certain degree of risk. We might need to drop the pretence of being completely in charge of everything in order to let go a little. At the heart of it is opening ourselves up to joy and hope, and also seeing the lightness of being at the heart of existence.

I learned much about mirth and merriment as I grew up and worked in my parents' small local hardware shop. We lived out these definitions. The most common sound wasn't the cash till – it was the sound of the kettle boiling and people laughing and chatting.

The shop was at the heart of the community and my parents' easy and happy ways made us a magnet for the lost and the lonely. What I remember is that I always felt I could be myself in the shop – something I never felt I could be at school. Perhaps that's the key to mirth and merriment: they help us to be relaxed enough to be ourselves. If a place or organization lets us be that, then it is getting something very right.

Mirth can be costly and is to be treasured

Mirth, it seems clear, is not a flimsy add-on to life. It is one of the things that makes it worth living and helps us to be the kind of person that brings love and joy to others. But do we treasure it enough?

THE QUEST BEGINS

The Jewish people are in captivity and are in deep mourning for all that they have lost. Perhaps we can all identify with the idea of a lost homeland of some kind.

They sit by the rivers of Babylon and weep for all that once was and is no longer. If only we could have what we once had. That is the spirit of the Psalm.

> By the rivers of Babylon we sat and wept
> when we remembered Zion.
> There on the poplars
> we hung our harps,
> for there our captors asked us for songs,
> our tormentors demanded songs of joy;
> they said, 'Sing us one of the songs of Zion!'
> How can we sing the songs of the Lord
> while in a foreign land?
>
> *Psalm 137:1–4*

There is an awful twist in the tail. The Jewish people are told to be merry and to sing their merry songs to entertain their captors and oppressors. We shudder when we think of the times this also happened in the concentration camps not that long ago right here in Europe.

They are forced to be merry or be punished, and that is a heavy weight to bear indeed. The Jewish people lament: 'How can we sing when we are in a foreign land?' It is a good question indeed.

I read this as both a historical fact and also as a comment on the nature of mirth. Sometimes we cannot summon mirth or the old songs when we feel oppressed or in a place that seems dangerous. It also speaks of how precious and fragile mirth and joy can be. They are gifts and we do well to cherish them when we are able to be in their presence and bring them to others. The psalm also reminds us that darkness can engulf us, and we feel unable to sing our mirthful 'songs' to the Lord. How do we praise him with laughter and song and merriment when we are oppressed on all sides?

We cannot take mirth and merriment for granted. They need nurturing and honouring and we must value them as part of the business of being alive and part of what makes us human beings.

The call to merriment is an ancient call

I don't think that I am alone in wanting more mirth and merriment – both in my life and in church and in the faith. It seems as though I am only the latest in a number of voices raised in the cause of livening things up a bit.

John Chrysostom was the archbishop of Constantinople in the fourth century. He asked that

THE QUEST BEGINS 19

the liturgy should become much more exciting. He complained that it was hard to grow the faith because the other faiths seemed to be more lively and fun and attractive. He noted that in the synagogue there was theatricality, with lyres and harps and drums. The synagogue even employed actors and dancers to make the services a truly merry and exciting time.[4]

It strikes me that the modern church faces similar competition but from the secular world. The sheer joy of a Zumba class in the church hall may put a traditional Sunday service in the shade.

Meeting a rabbi

I meet my rabbi friend in a café in north London. I'm wondering if I have missed some of the humour in the Holy Scriptures, some of the mirth and merriment. If I looked at it through Jewish eyes, might it be a bit funnier and a bit more mirthful?

He isn't all that encouraging. He tells me that the humour I find has a sting in the tail – it can be sarcastic. He looks concerned for me and a bit perplexed. He has a stack of books with him and has been poring over them.

Frank tells me that humour is part of Jewish life, and that it is also part of a particular tradition: laughing in the face of adversity. There is one joke shared especially during festivals that sums up not only a feisty spirit of defiance, but also a sheer love of food:

> They tried to kill us.
> But they failed.
> Now, let's eat.

Plus there are sayings and stories that Jews share to poke fun at themselves and even their revered biblical characters. For example, there's a rabbinic story that goes something like this: 'Abraham was supposed to be "Mr Hospitality". You know, his tent was always open in order to receive strangers. One day an idolater comes and wants a meal. Abraham is torn. What should he do? He turns to God and asks. God replies, "Come now, Abraham, I've had to put up with this idolater for seventy years and you're wondering whether or not to get him a meal?"' What is really important here is the ethic of extending non-judgemental hospitality to the stranger. (Fascinatingly, this story is also part of Islamic tradition.)

In Jewish life, it is the festivals that tend to generate merriment, especially Purim which is based on the story of Esther in the Apocrypha. Mirth and merriment may be in shortish supply in Scripture,

THE QUEST BEGINS

but they are part of Jewish life and their response to all that they have gone through. And there have been moments when the Jewish people have tried to recalibrate around something wildly joyous. Plus the sayings and wisdom of the Jewish people tends to point to a love of the good things in life. Take this: 'On Judgement Day, a man will have to give an account for every good thing which his eye saw and he did not enjoy.'

The Hasidim in the early eighteenth century were a radically pietistic movement. They tended to be anti-intellectual and worshipped God in an ecstatic and spontaneous way. They were joyful and mystical.

As we finish our coffees, Frank says, 'Look, we might find it hard to find much mirth in the holy books. Mirth is all about spontaneity, sharing, hospitality and the joy of being alive, even if life can be painful . . . There is something of God in all these things.'

The Gospels

The ground looks unpromising. The Gospels are dominated by the story of a horrific death. The church's first theologian (Paul) seemed to lack humour. He was sure that the end was nigh, and with that kind of world view, you tend to concentrate on action, not mirth. If time was precious and the world needed to be saved, then it was roll your sleeves up and get evangelizing. The church fathers tended to be obsessed with sin and the utter depravation of humanity. The organized church became corrupt and over-powerful, leading to the Reformation.

Church is not always fun. The Beatles' John Lennon admitted that when he was young, he gave up attending church when he was thrown out for laughing – by a vicar.[5]

There are glimmers, though. There is something simple and foolish about the faith. St Paul says as much (1 Cor. 2:14). The sophisticates in Athens could not take it seriously. The first-ever piece of graffiti depicts the Christ on the cross with a donkey head.[6] It was probably etched in the first century and showed that the Romans felt that the faith was a joke.

Christ's ministry starts with almost a pastoral edge. He walks around the lake, talking to people light-heartedly. He involves himself in some banter and wordplay and his first miracle is turning water into wine (John 2:1–12). Perhaps his disciples felt that they were in for a merry time, and indeed, there simply had to be merriment along the way. But the gospel stories are weighted towards the agonizing death of Christ and also his contending with various

THE QUEST BEGINS

people who oppose him. The mood becomes darker and darker. But I take hope from the fact that Christ's opponents called him a drunk and a 'glutton' (Luke 7:34) – which at least suggests that good times were part of the ministry.

Plus, some of the miracles have a comic turn. Taking a boy's packed lunch and providing mass catering was a neat turn (John 6:1–15). And because we only have the written word, we don't know Jesus' tone of voice and gestures, and this kind of thing can make all the difference. A wink or an arched eyebrow can put a whole new slant on things.

At the heart of mirth and merriment is the good news. That news is the possibility of something so deep that if we listen to what is on offer, then we are changed too. Joy is the currency. And, of course, we do hear frequent exhortations to be 'joyful' in the Bible (see for example Ps. 100:2; Rom. 12:12). It is as though it should be second nature, and perhaps we have just forgotten how to do it and be it.

Study questions

I revel in my congregation's eccentricities, and I sometimes find myself laughing during a service when something funny happens . . . I find church funny.

Can you think of any examples of eccentricities at church and how you react to them?

Perhaps a church that is too certain and unable to take itself and the faith and each other a little lightly is like the tree with shallow roots. Humour and mirth speak of a kind of freedom not to always see things as they are.

Is certainty the enemy of mirth? Do the churches you have gone to take themselves seriously?

Prayer

Lord, help us to seek out mirth and merriment and to see you at the heart of these. Help us to take a fresh look at your character and the simple mirth that marks you out. Help us to appreciate the lightness of church and the funny moments that happen.

3

The Mirth and Merriment I Grew Up With

Most of us, perhaps, trust that God has a sense of humour. Heaven without humour might seem a little dry. A diet of harp-strumming doesn't really appeal. I'd rather it involved a lovely pint of beer, friendship, singing and telling silly stories with the God who chose earthy and, no doubt, ribald fishermen and other disreputable folk to spend time with. I very much doubt that they minded their ps and qs.

What would life, or the afterlife, be like without humour? I have a feeling it would be like a world without birdsong, without music and without a sense of proportion. Humour is a bastion against scrupulousness, piety and extremism. Or at least, it should be.

Planted in humour

Humour is a way of getting things in proportion and getting a perspective on ourselves and our community. We all of us come with a mirth and merriment legacy from our upbringing. Our families and friends help us to find what is funny.

I was planted in a family that had humour at its core. I grew up in Northolt, which is at the very far west of London just before the greenbelt (or as we called it, scrubland) started. Northolt is the kind of place you have driven through before you have realized it is there. It is a mix of local authority and private houses. It has no cinema or theatre and no real centre. It is a place where people from the slums of the East End and Hammersmith spilled into after the war. It is easy to misjudge Northolt and many other places like it. For my parents, Northolt was the Promised Land – a place of newness and possibility. It was a place of safety where they could make a new life.

You might think today that it is a drab suburb, but that would be a mistake because our family, and many others, were alive with humour. They brought with them the humour they grew up with and the humour of the working communities they came from.

If I can understand something of this, I can see how church measures up.

The humour we grew up with was largely due to my father, who was an Eastender and brought with him that culture's attitude. When you mention Eastender, you might think 'Cockney', and from that it is a short jump to cheeky chappies cracking one-liners about being light-fingered. But the picture of East End humour is much more nuanced than that. Indeed, my grandmother, who lived over the road from us, *was* a Cockney, so we had both strands.

In my experience, East End humour very rarely involved actual jokes. In fact, I can't remember my East End family ever going in for jokes. Indeed, I have something of an aversion to jokes, unless they are silly and aren't aimed at people. Jokes are so often a cheap shot.

East End humour is intrinsically bound up with class and deprivation and surviving in a part of the world that was hostile and remorseless. The humour is an expression of class and a way of seeing beyond the life that people were forced to live. It is based on

THE MIRTH AND MERRIMENT

observation and comment – often turning a difficult issue or moment on its head.

We don't speak that much about class these days, but the Eastenders I grew up with were well aware of where they stood in the pecking order. Spending most of my life in my father's company, it seems to me that the humour he lived out every day was actually quite clearly focused. It had a purpose, and at times, it was all my dad had standing between him and chaos and despair.

My dad lost his father towards the end of the Second World War. It was the ultimate tragedy. His disabled mum was moved in with an abusive relative, and they all suffered. Later in life, Dad got motor neurone disease, and anyone who knows anything about that illness understands the bleakness at its heart.

Yet, no matter what, my father always had humour at his fingertips. The humour he lived out was a marker of family and community. The humorous tales of relatives and old friends and situations helped us to know where we came from and to feel a sense of identity. Jokes would have been and gone, but tales about life in the East End, and odd and endearing relatives, gave us a rich sense of the humour around my father's experience of being working class. It seems to me that humour is just this – a way of creating community. It certainly was in biblical times. The Jewish people used humorous tales – like the story of Jonah – to see themselves as a people and to revel in their idiosyncrasies. My father's stories, and those of my grandmothers, painted a picture of a tough life, but one with as much light as shade. I think that his humour owed a lot to his Jewish neighbours and employer in Canning Town.

Humour is also a way of healing the hurts that come in any life. Tragedy viewed through the lens of time can become comedy. My father would sometimes talk of the absurdity of the situation which followed him and his mum being bombed out during the war. The house was gone and they were injured. They had lost all their possessions. But my father said that at the moment of getting up from under the kitchen table, nearly deaf and amazed to be alive, they spotted that the only thing left in the kitchen was a cooker and a pan with an unbroken egg in the middle of being boiled.

> Tragedy viewed through the lens of time can become comedy.

A key plank of East End humour, and perhaps any humour from a minority, is the pricking of authority and pomposity. No figure of authority was safe.

Allied to this is tackling pride. East End humour thrives on knocking down its betters. This is the subversive side of humour and the side that dictators fear. Interestingly, Jesus uses just this technique on many occasions (e.g. Matt. 18:3).

At the heart of any effective humour is the belief that people are worthy of it and that people are funny. Also, life is, at times, ridiculous. Life is slapstick. There are times that we simply cannot help laughing, and in some way, that always feels liberating.

All this explains why I don't really like jokes. The humour I knew, growing up, was based on stories, on wit and on finding things silly – even when times were dark. It was a defence mechanism and a way of cementing family and friendships. It was a way of creating community and keeping it together. It was also cheap entertainment although it came at a price – the difficult lives that it effectively reshaped and recycled.

Back in 1959, Michael Young and Peter Willmott published an anthropological study of East London.[1] It is an interesting work that looks at patterns of life and kinship at a time when the old East End was about to change. Communities that had lived in the same crowded streets forever were breaking up – moving out to new council estates. A working-class community marked by hegemony was under strain.

Young and Willmott paint a picture of closeness. They explain the roles of matriarchs and patterns of employment. They look at the way the community has suffered and has struggled. They offer insights into what made this, and makes this, a community. But there is one thing they never mention – one enduring power that kept this community together through thick and thin. They never mention the humour of Eastenders and the way it is at the centre of kinship and family. In some communities, wearing a certain dress is a marker of belonging. For Eastenders, that marker is humour.

Read with the benefit of distance, the study seems patronizing – indeed, anthropological studies of this kind had fallen out of favour for just this reason. But I wonder, how could these eminent and well-educated researchers have missed the unique, sparkling humour of the people they studied? I wonder if it was because they felt the humour trivial, or perhaps too near-the-knuckle.

Perhaps some of us prefer a more genteel kind of humour to the full power and force that is on offer elsewhere. It is something that we must listen to as a church if we want a comeback for mirth. Mirth includes humour – and we are compelled, I think, to be open to broadening what is acceptable if we want to involve and include all parts of our community. Would God find the odd naughty joke or bold

THE MIRTH AND MERRIMENT

observation offensive? Jesus lived with fishermen. I guess he heard plenty of that stuff from them.

In that wonderful film *Stan & Ollie*,[2] there is a moment so poignant that the audience on the night I went to see it gasped. Spoiler alert! The two friends had a falling out and it was tough to be together. But they loved each other and their humour was priceless. The film features them on the skids – trying to resurrect their career on a tour of Britain's smaller venues. It is all too much for Ollie and he becomes ill and dies soon after.

As the film is ending, we read that Stan Laurel retreated to his home and for the rest of his life continued to write scripts for himself and his friend. This great comedy duo were parted by death, but humour and the love of entertaining each other and everyone else refused to die. Humour is, and was, more powerful than death. I wonder if many of us have the same feeling. I lost my father ten years ago, but sometimes I can still hear his voice. In certain circumstances a joke comes into my head that he would have cracked every time.

Just this week I saw a man walking past the church carrying a roll of carpet. At that moment there was my dad whispering to me, 'Hey, mate, are you taking your carpet for a walk?'

Merriment

Like many working-class families of the time, we enjoyed a good party. I don't mean dinner parties – we didn't do those. Maybe much later in my teens my parents had the odd dinner party, but that was a sign that they were moving up in the world. But we did often get together with friends, relatives and neighbours to share a bit of food, a drink and music.

As a boy, I loved these parties. I loved the way my dad would get the Union Jack from upstairs and we'd sing 'Land of Hope and Glory' together.

Everyone we knew voted Conservative and we were patriotic and loved the monarchy. We loved to have a good time and to simply have fun.

When my parents decided to try out church in the late 1970s, they went to the local Anglican one. They reported years later that they only went twice. On neither occasion did anyone talk to them and that everyone seemed cold and 'snooty'.

This observation still haunts me. I find it very sad – and also a warning.

I think what my parents sensed was a kind of middle-class reserve and piety that didn't play well with them. They were both exceptionally hard-working and respectable people, but church seemed dull and distant. They couldn't imagine the kind of kinship and fun happening there that they enjoyed in the street where we lived.

And so, I face a conundrum, or at least a question. Can church be a place with the kind of joy, happiness and fun that we enjoyed with our neighbours when I was a boy? I would like to think that it can be. But might we lose something holy if we did that? Might it be too boisterous, or even earthy? Are we more comfortable with polite and domesticated wit?

One of my friends has a church opposite the pub just around the corner from where I grew up in Northolt. I love what he is doing as it answers my question in the affirmative. What if we sometimes moved the church out of the building and worked on creating the kind of atmosphere and entertainment regular folk so often go in for?

A while back, I went to a pub quiz organized by St Mary's Church in Northolt by my old friend the Reverend Chris Hill. It was a brilliant evening and the quizzes are a huge success. Each month sixty to seventy people from my old hometown, Northolt, would meet at the pub for the quiz organized by the church. Chris was in his clerical collar and the quiz was a thing of great joy and fun. It wasn't too difficult, which helps, and wasn't overrun with 'professional' quizzers.

Before Covid-19, the pub was at the heart of Northolt life – always had been. Chris realized this and unleashed a creative ministry centred on it. Why not? The pub, right over the road from the church, was a pleasant and welcoming place.

Each week he ran a very successful memory café at the pub. This was a wonderful thing. The pub was warm and opened up an hour early each week for the café. The café grew and became part of a vibrant offering to the people of Northolt. It had great advantages for the church, of course. The pub was paying for the heating, which always helps. But the pub benefited too as the centre of the community – not just a place to drink in.

Chris also had a Christmas dinner at the pub for the congregation, and other events too.

Sure, there was loads going on at the church. But what I liked most was that Chris and his team were developing a really interesting community ministry. They were going to the people, where they already were, and signalling that Christians are just like everyone else.

One of St Mary's values is that what they do should be *fun*. That is a great organizational value and one we

THE MIRTH AND MERRIMENT

could all adopt. I want to have fun. I think that God loves fun too. There is surely a reason that Jesus' first miracle was to turn water into wine (John 2:1–12) and not the other way round. Of course, excess alcohol consumption is a terrible burden on families. But based on my experience in Northolt, no one was there to drink themselves silly. Maybe, after the coronavirus pandemic, more churches could utilize their local pub as a centre of local events and, even if subtly, a place of evangelism and connection. It might be a very short hop from a quiz to giving church a try.

Mirth and merriment and class

Perhaps I have been skirting a problematic issue. Class. I grew up in a working-class family and the patterns of mirth and merriment stem largely from that. But working-class mirth and merriment are often felt to be suspicious, unstable and dangerous. Anyone can laugh and you don't need lessons in it. As Terry Eagleton points out,[3] laughter is unlike more middle-class areas of expertise – like leaning to play the cello. It requires no expertise, and it is a threat to power sometimes. Gentle wit and clever satire are somehow safer and more exclusive.

So, if we are interested in building a church of mirth and humour, we may need to prepare ourselves for an experience that is less controlled, refined and safe.

Study questions

Humour is a way of getting things in proportion and getting a perspective on ourselves and our community. We all of us come with a mirth and merriment legacy from our upbringing. Our families and friends help us to find what is funny.

What is the mirth legacy that you have, and how has this affected your life?

What if we sometimes moved the church out of the building and worked on creating the kind of atmosphere and entertainment regular folk so often go in for?

Consider this question carefully. What do *you* think might happen?

So, if we are interested in building a church of mirth and humour, we may need to prepare ourselves for an experience that is less controlled, refined and safe.

Are we prepared to take this risk?

Prayer

Thank you for the humour we grew up with. Let us be grateful for it, and also to be discerning about how we use it. Help us to grow in our humour, acknowledge our influences and let you shape just the right way of showing mirth for those who hear us.

PART TWO

The Theology of Mirth

4

The Comedy Slackers

When you are working hard, the last thing that you need is a slacker who turns up towards the end of the day – and then the boss decides to pay them a full day's wage. As a businessman once said to me, 'I'd go bust if I did that here.'

Exactly. The 'foolishness of God' (1 Cor. 1:25) is not really a good advert for sensible economics. But the story isn't really about how to run a business. Instead, it's about God's kingdom and how different it is to the world as it is. It is about how unfair grace is – but it's as though God says, 'Deal with it!'

THE COMEDY SLACKERS

Let's look at the story. It comes in Matthew 20:1–16 and concludes with one of the greatest teachings of Jesus.

Christ is speaking about one of his favourite subjects – the kingdom of heaven. What is it going to be like? It is something even those who say they don't believe seem quite interested in. So, what is heaven like? Well, we know it is the kind of place where the usual rules seem to be torn up.

The landowner pays the wages for his daily workers. A full day's work gets you a denarius. That's fair enough. It is hot work and physically demanding. He recruits some workers early on and then recruits more at intervals during the day. He doesn't say how much he will pay the late starters, just that he will be fair with them (v. 4) – which is, of course, a great divine joke, because he is going to be more than fair – profligate, in fact. He even recruits some workers when most of the work is done. This is the exchange:

> About five in the afternoon he went out and found still others standing around. He asked them, 'Why have you been standing here all day long doing nothing?'
>
> 'Because no one has hired us,' they answered.

> 'He said to them, 'You also go and work in my vineyard.'
>
> *vv. 6,7*

The men wanted to work but no one had picked them. Perhaps they had reputations as slackers or troublemakers. At the end of the day the owner of the vineyard calls all the men together. He pays the ones hired last, first.

When the ones who have been working all day come for their money, they get just the same as the latecomers:

> When they received it, they began to grumble against the landowner. 'These who were hired last worked only one hour,' they said, 'and you have made them equal to us who have borne the burden of the work and the heat of the day.'
>
> *vv. 11,12*

We might feel a bit sorry for those who had been labouring all day. How can this be fair? The landowner answers the question:

> 'I am not being unfair to you, friend. Didn't you agree to work for a denarius? Take your pay and go. I want to give the one who was hired last the same as I gave you. Don't I have the right to do

THE COMEDY SLACKERS

what I want with my own money? Or are you envious because I am generous?'

So the last will be first, and the first will be last.

vv. 13–16

It is rather beautiful, and I think if you had been one of those workers hired at 5 p.m. then all you'd be able to do would be to laugh – to be full of mirth and merriment. 'How did that happen? We've only been here an hour and we got the same pay as everyone else.'

It is so foolish and so ludicrously generous that you'd have a smile on your face for days on end. It isn't, of course, that the Lord dragged you unwillingly from your bed. You wanted to work, but you weren't in the in-crowd. And so the pay is not just fair, it is astounding.

You might not be so mirthful if you had been slaving away all day. But you got a fair wage . . . it's just that those who didn't look like they deserved it got a pay-out as well.

But in the final analysis it is both comedy economics and the best news there can be. It is the kind of news that would mean you could relax and enjoy your life and spread as much joy and merriment as you could. We are all slackers; we none of us really deserve grace. But it is on offer even to those who appear to be coming in last.

If the Christian faith is not propelling us to celebration, then we need to wonder whether we have got God wrong. If 'the last will be first', then we do need to reappraise what success is and what rewards are on offer. If those who got the same pay as the latecomers only realized it, then the joke is not going to be on them.

The next day, *they* might be the workers waiting for hours in the sun for a day's work. They would then be only too happy to accept God's gift. And they might get a sense of God, not as a forbidding presence in the sky, but the creator of life who is so generous that even those who don't deserve it are pushed centre stage.

The latecomers, though, might get the wrong end of the stick. We can imagine them sniggering that they had got away without working. That the mugs who were there all day did no better in terms of pay than they did. But the parable isn't about slackers getting away with it, it is about God who puts his dignity behind him and does something that seems to make no sense and would make even the most hardened old vineyard-worker smile.

> That's what heaven looks like. It will be full of latecomers.

That's what heaven looks like. It will be full of latecomers, the last in line and the slackers. That is quite funny really.

Study questions

The 'foolishness of God' . . . is not really a good advert for sensible economics.

What do you think of this? What does it say about the nature of God?

If the Christian faith is not propelling us to celebration, then we need to wonder whether we have got God wrong. If 'the last will be first', then we do need to reappraise what success is and what rewards are on offer. If those who got the same pay as the latecomers only realized it, then the joke is not going to be on them.

Why is the Christian faith uniquely able to offer a sense of celebration and merriment?

That's what heaven looks like. It will be full of latecomers, the last in line and the slackers.

If 'the last will be first', how might we view those around us?

Prayer

Help us to live out your teaching about the last being first. Help us to reorder our priorities now and think about our mission and vision for church. Let us see the enormous mirth and 'silliness' in your ways and rejoice in them.

5

Creation Laughs

Something tells me that mirth and merriment might be hardwired into the universe itself. I can agree that God might have made the world for fun, that he did it as an act of joy, just because he could. I can see that we might have a completely different view of Jesus if we were surrounded by religious art featuring him laughing and smiling.

But when we read those ancient Jewish songs and prayers, the Psalms, we hear a rumour that creation itself is in a good mood. It helps that Psalm 42 tells us that God himself sings (v. 8). Creation itself is so packed with joy at the presence and influence of the Creator that it is 'glad'! And gladness is often one of the ingredients of mirth and certainly merriment. The language is astounding, and the images are powerful:

> Let the heavens rejoice, let the earth be glad;
> let the sea resound, and all that is in it.
> Let the fields be jubilant, and everything in them;
> let all the trees of the forest sing for joy.
> Let all creation rejoice before the Lord ...
>
> *Psalm 96:11–13*

The trees of the forest are singing. Perhaps they are singing still, if only we had ears to hear. It is as though a huge party is going on. If we just heard this once, it would be an eye-opener. But the same theme is picked up on other occasions. If we were able to listen, we might be able to hear the trees and the seas and the fields bursting forth in song and joy and merriment:

> The grasslands of the wilderness overflow;
> the hills are clothed with gladness.
> The meadows are covered with flocks
> and the valleys are mantled with corn;
> they shout for joy and sing.
>
> *Psalm 65:12,13*

CREATION LAUGHS

We should be able to hear because creation is shouting at the top of its metaphorical lungs. It is a view of an animated creation. It is not just a creation struggling for survival of the fittest. The trees know something of their creator and are glad. They 'clap their hands', as Isaiah 55:12 informs us.

> The trees know something of their creator and are glad.

Isaiah is the book Christ would have known by heart. He quotes it more often than any other source. He was soaked through in its logic and law. And so he would have been familiar with the verse which follows. Perhaps more than familiar; perhaps he loved it.

> You will go out in joy
> and be led forth in peace;
> the mountains and hills
> will burst into song before you,
> and all the trees of the field
> will clap their hands.
> Instead of the thorn-bush will grow the juniper,
> and instead of briers the myrtle will grow.
> This will be for the Lord's renown,
> for an everlasting sign,
> that will endure for ever.
>
> *Isaiah 55:12,13*

Christ is about to enter Jerusalem, which will be the scene of his apparent defeat – the end of the mission to save the world. The crowds are cheering him. The religious authorities – the killers of joy and mirth – are pursuing him with questions, as ever.

The Pharisees have a strict message: 'Stop these people celebrating you!' But Jesus knows something that the religious types don't know. He knows that joy in the company of the God who is with us cannot be contained. Whatever the world has to throw at him, or us, the world of matter is in on the secret.

> When he came near the place where the road goes down the Mount of Olives, the whole crowd of disciples began joyfully to praise God in loud voices for all the miracles they had seen:
>
> 'Blessed is the king who comes in the name of the Lord!'
>
> 'Peace in heaven and glory in the highest!'
>
> Some of the Pharisees in the crowd said to Jesus, 'Teacher, rebuke your disciples!'
>
> 'I tell you,' he replied, 'if they keep quiet, the stones will cry out.'
>
> *Luke 19:37–40*

I hope that the stones are crying out still, and that one day I will join all of creation in the never-ending song of glory and praise. That when my life ends here it will only really be beginning. I am from East End stock – I love a party.

Creation and the mirth of God

Jesus created the world, but why might he want to do it? If we accept that the Trinity is complete and completely self-sufficient in itself, then the act of creation was done simply because they could and they did.

When we begin to wonder whether God has a sense of humour, we need to go right back to the roots of this act of creation. When we think about it, the creation is both astounding and unnecessary. God did not need to create anything – least of all us. He did it because he could.

This puts a rather beautiful spin on the creation. God made the world for fun – as an act of spontaneity and joy. We certainly hear that he found what he had created 'good', as we read Genesis 1. But what we might take from it is that we are a product of divine carefreeness and that there might be a keen sense of humour behind and within creation.

By making the universe and all the galaxies and everything, God shows that he delights in *things*, in matter. This helps us to combat any idea of God as simply cerebral. God created matter, real stuff, and the interaction between us and the real stuff around us is the very basis of most humour. It is an essential part of humour.

Comedy is a kind of wonderment. It often works by seeing the things around us in a different way, and in so doing, helps us to see the wonder in things again.

When we contemplate the terrors and pains of existence and the picture of a world that after creation rapidly fell, then both us and our world seem like a poor and failed experiment. But if the Trinity created the world out of creativity and joy, and even a sense of fun, then we see reflections of these everywhere and gain tremendous hope in them.

If creation has an attitude and propensity to mirth, then it might point to something at the heart of creation itself.

If we read the Genesis accounts of creation, we see that God seems to have a good deal of playfulness along the way. Rather than create everything at once, he takes his time, crafting new things every day and seemingly taking great pleasure in this.

He takes a day off at the end – perhaps not just to rest, but to enjoy his creation too. And of course, we hear that what God created he found to be good and pleasing (Gen. 1:31 – 2:3).

Perhaps creation is merry because the Creator is merry as well. Perhaps the cry of creation is a deep joy – and we know that joy and playfulness tend to hold hands.

Study questions

Creation itself is so packed with joy at the presence and influence of the Creator that it is 'glad'!

How does this strike you? Does it give you a different view of the nature of the created world?

The trees know something of their creator and are glad. They 'clap their hands' . . .

If creation is in a state of merriment, how does that help us to get more of a perspective on our own lives?

If we read the Genesis accounts of creation, we see that God seems to have a good deal of playfulness along the way. Rather than create everything at once, he takes his time, crafting new things every day and seemingly taking great pleasure in this.

Reflect on why God may have wanted to create the world. What was his attitude to the task?

Prayer

Thank you for the beautiful idea and image of creation celebrating and being merry. Would you help us to celebrate along with it?

6

Jesus and Humour

Wonder and foolishness

The wonder we feel, when we think of God and see his creation, is a source of joy and mirth and points us to God. Foolishness followed Jesus around – or more to the point, many people at the time felt that he and his message were foolish (Luke 16:14). He spoke about odd and bizarre things – like the out-of-control seed thrower (Matt. 13:1–8), scattering precious seeds everywhere, and the king who invited those outside on the street to a wedding

JESUS AND HUMOUR

celebration rather than the great and the good (Matt. 22:9,10).

So, when we read the Gospels and search for mirth and merriment, we need to bear these aspects of God in mind. If we don't always find what we are looking for, we need to take a step back and wonder about the nature of God and his creation. If we see there are signs and clues of the merriment of the Trinity, then that is, at least, a start.

Jesus and laughter

One of the questions that has bothered me over the years is whether Jesus had a sense of humour. It troubles me that we do not once hear that Jesus laughed, although we do hear that he wept (John 11:35). I am not alone, I am sure, in wishing that we had seen much more evidence of the divine chuckle – although all that I said above, I hope, means that we can at least recognize a sense of mirth in the DNA of creation.

> One of the questions that has bothered me over the years is whether Jesus had a sense of humour.

One thing that works against us discerning humour in Jesus' ministry is that we have no idea from the

Bible text the tone of voice he adopts. Often an inflection can make all the difference in how we hear what is being said. But that, alas, we do not have the luxury of.

However, anyone who knows how to weep knows how to laugh. The two go together. In some ways, they are the same thing – both a loss of control, both a response to circumstances and both an expression of an emotion. What's more, sometimes the things that seem so tragic, given time, can reveal elements of comedy that we may have thought were impossible.

The issue of the Lord's mirth exercised one of the greatest writers on the faith, G.K. Chesterton. Chesterton was jolly, and people loved him for it. His laugh was infectious, and he had a way of not taking himself seriously. He was absent-minded, and his affairs were a bit of a mess. He was likeable.

But the public persona hid much tragedy. While recovering from a breakdown, Chesterton wrote one of his best books, *Orthodoxy*.[1] It is a rather chaotic affair, perhaps reflecting the inner chaos of the author's emotional life at the time. Chesterton's mind turns to the question of mirth – something he himself felt in short supply of at the time. He wrestles with whether Jesus laughed and, in the end, can only manage the idea that he did so in private.

JESUS AND HUMOUR

Chesterton seeks to solve the conundrum of the laughter-free God who was man by wondering if he kept his mirth hidden. Perhaps when Jesus was in his quiet time with his Father, they laughed. Perhaps. But his humour is on view if we just choose to look.

There are reasons why we may miss the humour of Jesus. We tend to think that religion is a serious business. We don't immediately think of comic banter when we think of church (although Jesus was an expert at banter himself). Another reason we don't spot the humour is that so much of the Gospels is about the tragedy of the crucifixion and the events before it. Most religious art concentrates on the momentous events of the cross – so it's not surprising we lack images of the laughing and smiling Christ. But how might the faith be different, how much more appealing, if we had art that pictured the God who made the universe having a good giggle?

Perhaps also we need to understand the context in which the Gospels were written. A writer such as Mark was possibly facing his own execution and had to write quickly with just the main messages. The fact that this gospel ends mid-sentence holds open the prospect that Mark was scribbling down his words as he waited to be dragged from his cell. In these circumstances, adding the jokes of Jesus might seem superfluous.

If we delve a bit, we do see many examples of the strange humour of Jesus. And we can see that his sense of humour is very personal and individual to him, rather than just the standard markers of Old Testament humour – a love of irony and puns. With careful reading we see a very unique sense of humour that rings true. It isn't laugh-out-loud funny, but that isn't to say there weren't many moments like this which just weren't reported.

There are other reports that help us. We know that Jesus liked to hang out with sinners – eating and drinking. He had a reputation for fun – his enemies called him a 'glutton and a drunkard' (Luke 7:34), as we noted earlier. So we can say that he probably spent a good deal of time eating and drinking.

One of the elements of the humour of Christ is his use of the device of turning the world round the wrong way (something that is in the repertoire of most clowns) and so making people think again. Take the baptism of Jesus. John the Baptist understands that Jesus' request for baptism is irregular, to say the least. He says: 'I need to be baptised by you, and do you come to me?' (Matt. 3:14). Christ is without sin; he does not need to be baptized. But he does so anyway. Why? To stand alongside sinners and identify himself with us and to identify with spiritual struggle. And also, it has an edge of upside-down humour about it.

Christ's baptism is a comedic announcement of the odd upside-down nature of the kingdom of God where the last are first. It showed that now things would not be as they had been. In modern parlance, John the Baptist would have said, 'Me, baptize you? You've got to be joking!'

With our antennae tuned, we begin to see the humour of Jesus everywhere. Walking by the Sea of Galilee, he comes across two fishermen casting their nets. He goes up to them and says, 'Come, follow me . . . and I will send you out to fish for people' (Matt. 4:19). Yes, it's a pun, but it's a good one and probably counts as Rabbi Jesus' first joke.

When he meets up with Nathanael, Jesus engages in something that looks suspiciously like banter (John 1:45–51) – perhaps the kind of thing everyday folk and fishermen of the times would have specialized in. Nathanael quips that perhaps nothing very good can come out of Nazareth. When they meet, Jesus gives a rather funny, ringing endorsement: 'Here truly is an Israelite in whom there is no deceit.' To get that joke, you have to know that 'Israel' was Jacob – whose name can mean 'deceiver'. You can imagine

Jesus saying this, poker-faced. Nathanael hails Jesus as the 'Son of God', which is odd and perhaps a challenge. Jesus quips back, 'You believe because I told you I saw you under the fig-tree.'

This is undeniably evidence of humour on the part of Jesus. It is the kind of humour that sees Jesus giving his accident-prone friend and follower, Simon, a new name (John 1:42). He will no longer be Simon, the simple fisherman. Instead, he will be Cephas (or 'Peter'), which means 'rock'. There can be no less rock-like person in the Bible. Peter needs to be liked, puts his foot in it and consistently misspeaks. And yet, Jesus names him Rocky. It is delicious. It is a name he might not quite be able to live up to, but perhaps it's the thought that counts. In a way the delicious irony of it will mean perhaps all concerned treat Peter's later failure with sympathy.

In Jesus' teaching we see a return again and again to the same kinds of motifs and approaches. Jesus washes the feet of his disciples (John 13:1–17), turning the world upside down. Jesus uses the language of exaggeration – camels going 'through the eye of a needle' (Mark 10:25).

There is a cartoon edge to some of Jesus' images. The image of the person with the large plank of wood in their eye commenting on the tiny speck in the eye of another (Matt. 7:3–5) could come out of any of the cartoon greats.

These facets of Christ's humour serve a purpose and also let us see him as a real flesh-and-blood person. Christ's humour is full of the last being first. It is full of the puncturing of pomposity. It is playful and uses language to shrink what is large and enlarge what is small.

But we need to tackle another issue of Christ's humour that is less comfortable. Sometimes the things Christ said were offensive. He calls the Pharisees 'vipers' (Matt. 23:33), he calls his friend Peter 'Satan' (Matt. 16:23). Jesus doesn't hold back at times. In our polite ways we might not have the same boldness with name-calling. Indeed, in our sensitive times, Jesus' directness might not pass any 'safe-space' test. What are we to make of it?

It certainly doesn't seem to be a licence to lace our humour, our conversations, with insults. Jesus was often tender and didn't simply jump in. His 'insults' were rare and in context and part of a culture where this kind of thing was part of everyday discourse. What it probably says is that something simply being insulting is not necessarily a marker that it shouldn't be said.

It is a challenging idea. What we can be relatively certain of is that if Christ were truly a person just like us, then he must have had a sense of mirth.

Beyond laughter

Perhaps there is a deeper insight and signal of Christ's mirth. His ministry was full of tender and intimate friendships with both men and women. Indeed, Christ's encouragement and gentleness with women was in sharp contrast to the way the society generally treated them. When Christ sees his friend Mary weeping over the death of Lazarus, he too weeps (John 11:33–35). His was a life-giving intimacy and must have extended to all of those he met and travelled with. He healed the woman with the embarrassing gynaecological issue and made her not embarrassed (Luke 8:43–48). He listened and spoke with the outcast woman at the well (John 4:1–42). He stuck with his disciples. He welcomed people into the circle of his gentle, light-hearted friendship. He showed abundant tenderness to the widow whose only son had died (Luke 7:11–15).

The gentleness and love of the God who was friendly surely point to the gamut of behaviours associated with that. Christ put people at their ease. His lovely friendship, welcome and acceptance must have been a huge call to mirth and merriment. Good news, God is with us, likes us, and is gentle and beautiful.

Study questions

Chesterton seeks to solve the conundrum of the laughter-free God who was man by wondering if he kept his mirth hidden. Perhaps when Jesus was in his quiet time with his Father, they laughed. Perhaps.

Does this explanation by Chesterton ring true? Did Jesus hide his humour out of a sense of modesty?

There is a cartoon edge to some of Jesus' images. The image of the person with the large plank of wood in their eye commenting on the tiny speck in the eye of another . . . could come out of any of the cartoon greats.

Can you think of other examples of the humour of Jesus?

Christ put people at their ease. His lovely friendship, welcome and acceptance must have been a huge call to mirth and merriment.

Have you ever thought about what it must have been like for the disciples (and others), to spend time with Jesus as a friend? Does this picture change any of your ideas about what Christ was like as he walked on earth?

Prayer

Lord, can you help us to see the mirth and merriment of Jesus and forgive us that we see him as such a sombre figure? We want to see our Lord in all his facets! One of these is an ability to laugh and not to take ourselves too seriously.

7

The Incarnation

The incarnation and mirth

It is the incarnation that sets the Christian faith apart. Christianity makes the breathtaking, even foolish, claim that God took human form, that he was one of us. In fact, he still takes human form, even having ascended into heaven. We hear that his hands and feet still bear the wounds of his earthly suffering (Luke 24:39,40) and so we understand that Christ is still embodied.

Jesus is God in human form. We hear that he was 'tempted . . . just as we are' (Heb. 4:15). We hear that he wept when his friend died (John 11:35). It is frustrating that we don't hear about his laugh and what made him mirthful. But just because we have an absence of this, the sheer logic of the incarnation means that he must have had mirth and that his humour and lightness were part of who he was.

Without these qualities he would have seemed odd – like someone pretending to be a person and not the real deal. So, why does mirth and merriment have to be part of the incarnation?

Mirth, humour and merriment truly mark out the human species. They are what makes life bearable; they help people to heal from trauma and they comment on the unfairness and difficulties of life. The incarnation means that Christ lived everyday life, and we can't get through that without mirth. When God finished creating the world, he saw that it was 'very good' (Gen. 1:31). It is still good and part of that goodness is the propensity towards carefree jollity.

So when we think of the mystery and madness of the incarnation we should be drawn to the inevitability of mirth. We would be a horror to ourselves

THE INCARNATION

and to others without mirth and merriment – and so would Christ have been.

More about Jesus

> When we see the humour of Christ, I think that we warm to him.

When we see the humour of Christ, I think that we warm to him. The examples in the last chapter, at least, help us to challenge the notion that Christ had no sense of humour – that he never laughed.

James Cary in *The Sacred Art of Joking* points out that Jesus and his disciples spent months with each other, in close company. They must have joked with each other – teased and shared funny stories.[1]

It is also a doorway into the mystery and beauty of the incarnation. We may not read reports of Jesus laughing, but that does not mean that he did not laugh often and heartily. It does not mean that he watched his disciples with a dispassionate eye. Perhaps he found them hilarious. Maybe he revelled in the funny things that happened when people crowded around him. It may simply mean that portraying his humour and wit wasn't the priority of the writers of the Gospels.

Would Christ have been the kind of leader he clearly was if he did not have a sense of humour and jollity? Would people have followed him if he was a dry old stick? I have to answer a resounding 'no' to both.

The incarnation makes no sense if Christ lacked a sense of humour and indeed encouraged such a thing in the others around him. I want life to have been a riot when Jesus was around, and the absence of evidence of this in the Bible won't stop me wanting this. The evidence of his interactions with people make it more, rather than less, likely.

And there is the evidence of the presence of tragedy in Christ's life. We know that Jesus wept when his friend died, and we also know that he felt abandoned by God as he faced the reality of the cross. If he had these emotional responses in his repertoire, he must also have had jollity and humour as well. They are bedfellows.

God and mirth, foolishness and jollity

So, where are we with Jesus and humour? We never hear that he laughed, but that is no guarantee that he was laugh-free. Indeed, simple logic points us to the laughing Messiah. It's just that almost all religious art paints him without a smile on his face.

THE INCARNATION

How much more amazing would it be if we were to imagine God with a smile and a joke on his lips and a twinkle in his eye?

We can probably tick all three of our key words in relation to Jesus – mirth, foolishness and jollity. If we do that then we can begin to look for places where there has been an outbreak of such verities in the church and ponder how a modern church might take them on.

The mission of Jesus looked like a fool's errand. In some ways, it still does. It was fraught with risk and frequently turned the accepted way of looking at things on its head. Jesus had a sense of humour – although it has been ignored. To inspire people in the way he did, he could not have operated by fear. And, of course, the Keystone Cops antics of the disciples (think Peter opening mouth and inserting foot) must have made for rich comedy at the time.

This is all very challenging. For those of a serious disposition, the church with mirth, foolishness and jollity at its heart may seem lightweight and even worrying. We have all been on the end of horrible and nasty humour, and so we are a bit suspicious of it in a church context, perhaps. What if all that results from it is a terrible joke or two at the start of a sermon? That would be thin fare.

Perhaps, though, the call is deeper and builds on the way Jesus used wit along with wisdom. We are aware of the tragedy at the heart of Jesus' life – the cross. But comedy is always tragedy's bedfellow, and so perhaps we might probe at least, and wonder, what a faith orientated around things that make us laugh and smile might look like.

Jesus tells us something important

In the Gospel of John (16:33) Jesus says something that is profound and easy to miss. He says:

> But take heart! I have overcome the world.
> *John 16:33*

On the one hand, it is a good instruction for us to be merry. That doesn't mean to always have a smile on our face. But on the other, it means that we have a propensity, a default-setting towards mirth and cheer. We can take this as a description of Christ's own character. We may not get much outright mirth in the Gospels, but we can guess at least that being with Jesus was heartening.

THE INCARNATION

What would that have looked like? One imagines times of fun and joking. Perhaps they mucked around at times and were silly. Perhaps they reflected on their interactions with others and found them sweet and affecting. Even as they prepared for Christ's death, I hope that they all had time to enjoy each other's company – to enjoy their meals and stories.

The second part of the quotation is fascinating. Christ says to 'take heart' because the world and all the obstacles it has to offer cannot get the better of us. If we take a perspective based on eternity, then we begin to see the funnier side of life. The idea seems to be that we are both of the world and also in transition from it. If this is so, then our story is even more wonderful than we ever imagined. That is bound to put a smile on anyone's face.

Jesus' claim is quite specific. We can 'take heart' – other versions, such as the nkjv have 'good cheer' – because he has 'overcome the world'. We are set free for thankfulness because the incarnated God was able to transcend the bitter, existential bleakness that we can feel without him. He recasts the nature of reality and places 'good cheer' at the heart of it.

If this is so, then we might begin to wonder how we recreate this in our incarnated lives, in our families, relationships and in church. Perhaps we should do an audit each year to see how much 'good cheer' we have experienced in church.

The kingdom of God is near

Christ was, perhaps, at his most enigmatic when he spoke about the kingdom of God being near (Luke 21:31). His listeners weren't all that sure what to make of this – I wonder if we are any surer.

The incarnation made a statement that heaven and earth are far closer than anyone had ever thought. Indeed, when we see the sweep of the Christ story, we realize that the coming kingdom is already in motion – something of our daily lives is caught up in the sweep of history which heads in only one direction.

Jesus lived out some of that near-kingdom life. He also spoke about what the kingdom is like (e.g. Mark 4:26; Mark 4:30; Luke 13:18) and it truly is rather wonderful, and at least one of our responses must be merriment – as well as a second, mirth.

The picture of the kingdom drawn in Christ's parables is a riot of profligacy, banquets and making sure never to store up too much wealth. It features the carefreeness of the birds (Matt. 6:26). It features

THE INCARNATION

a king who invites the riff-raff to a party (Matt. 22:9,10). Christ's miracles feature a very handy water-into-wine and walking on water (John 2:1–12; John 6:16–21). As well as raising an old friend from the dead (John 11:1–44).

Many at the time probably thought Christ's message was foolish. The kingdom of God that is near, and here around us, is no bureaucracy or dictatorship. Its rules throw our rules on their head.

It is preposterous. Thank God. And that is a cause to smile and celebrate.

Celebrate lives – but how?

The incarnation adds a touch of holiness to every life. If Christ was one of us, then our own lives seem to matter. There is something godly about life itself. And perhaps this points us in a whole new direction when we come to celebrate a life that's been lived.

Perhaps when we tell the story of a person who has died – in a eulogy, either formal or informal – we shouldn't leave out the funny, annoying and strange parts. If we celebrate the whole thing, then mirth has to break through, and that can break the spell of sadness.

If we mention the person's annoying habits, then we do so because in some odd way they seem funny and we miss them being annoying. We mention that they always left their socks on the floor and we can laugh at it – celebrate it. Perhaps Jesus left his clothes all over the place as well. After all, when he is resurrected, his clothes are neatly stacked in the empty tomb (John 20:6,7). Perhaps an angel did it – folded them up and put them neatly in a pile!

Study questions

Without [humour and lightness Jesus] would have seemed odd – like someone pretending to be a person and not the real deal. So, why does mirth and merriment have to be part of the incarnation?

Why do you think that Christ was likely to have been surrounded by mirth? What would he have been like without it?

This is all very challenging. For those of a serious disposition, the church with mirth, foolishness and jollity at its heart may seem lightweight and even worrying.

Where do you think that line between seriousness and mirth should lie?

Jesus' claim is quite specific. We can . . . have 'good cheer' – because he has 'overcome the world'. We are set free for thankfulness because the incarnated God was able to transcend the bitter, existential bleakness that we can feel without him. He recasts the nature of reality and places 'good cheer' at the heart of it.

How does Christ recast reality? What would life look like if mirth seemed godly and natural?

Prayer

We thank you for the mystery and majesty of the incarnation. Help us to see the way mirth and merriment were key parts of your mission to save the world. Help us to love out of the precious ministry of mirth.

PART THREE

Outbreaks of Mirth and Merriment

8

Politics, Fools and Speaking into Power

I think that we might all agree that mirth (including humour) can be a good way of puncturing the delusions of the pompous – be that a person or institution. This kind of puncturing is at the heart of a great deal of humour. Perhaps we might also agree that mirth is healthy and healing. It is a great tonic. But can mirth have any impact on, say, the politics or direction of a nation? Is it a powerful weapon? If we had laughed more often at the vanities, inanities and powerful, might history have been different?

POLITICS, FOOLS AND SPEAKING   83

That great journalist and essayist E.B. White, in his introduction to a book on American humourists, noted that while the court fool of Shakespeare's time was a minnow on the social scale, they did get the attention of the powerful. Narrative poets at court were glamorous – the film stars of their day. But the fool was able to give the monarch good advice and that counted for something. White urges the world to pay much more attention to nonsense.[1]

In March 1929, the Chicago Forum Council[2] announced that it was to host a debate between W.E.B. Du Bois, a prominent black intellectual, and Lothrop Stoddard, a historian/journalist white supremacist. The debate was to explore whether black people should seek cultural equality. Stoddard was a popularist and, as a journalist, employed a neat turn of phrase.

The audience was mainly black and may have numbered as many as 5,000 people with many unable to get in on the night. Most of the debate was made up of Stoddard making various claims for white supremacy, each batted back by Du Bois. Stoddard trotted out the ideas explained in Madison Grant's books (Grant was also an acclaimed conservationist) asserting that a white master race was in danger of being swamped. Grant's book *The Passing of the*

Great Race[3] was a bestseller and was an influence on Adolf Hitler.

The debate was orderly. But there was a moment when things turned. Stoddard spoke of the virtues of bi-racialism. He explained that each race should have its own public sphere and that in the South this was already happening. Separating the races was not about discrimination at all, they were aiming to ensure that even if the black people had separate trains, they should be good trains.

In the notes of the debate there is a single word at this point in brackets. It seems that laughter broke out.

The mainly black audience knew that the rail carriages, known as Jim Crow cars, set aside for them were vile and filthy, and no thinking person would ever choose to travel in them. Stoddard had shown the ridiculous underbelly of his arguments. What he said had no relation to reality.

What actually happened was that laughter broke out in all parts of the hall. To make things worse, or better, Stoddard said he couldn't see what was funny. This generated even more laughter. Stoddard was not able to recover and soon after the debate ended. He never agreed to debate with Du Bois again.

POLITICS, FOOLS AND SPEAKING 85

It is a sweet story and says something of the power of laughter to puncture. But it is also a horrible warning on the limits of laughter. More horrors were in store for the black people of America. Du Bois's old home in the Bronx is now a parking lot. He died at a ripe old age the day before the March on Washington in August 1963. Stoddard ended up as a Nazi supporter and apologist and died in obscurity in 1950.

The laughter in the hall was perhaps more prophetic than a signal of immediate change. The laughter was a comment on the world as it was and the preposterous notions that it lived out. But the laughter aimed at Stoddard was a voice calling in the wilderness (see Matt. 3:3). It would take other weapons and other strategies for society to move on and tackle the injustices of racism. Indeed, we might say that that battle is still in its infancy.

I wonder where we might find evidence of that prophetic and powerful laughter against those who monopolize power and oppress the people. Perhaps when God visits a series of plagues on the man, the pharaoh, oppressing his people back in the book of Exodus – this has a comic edge. Why send flies and frogs and boils when you could just click your fingers and obliterate the dictator? Was it God laughing at the pretentions of the dictator?

Laughter and the power of the church

In Umberto Eco's book *The Name of the Rose*,[4] the vexed issue of laughter arises. One monk, Jorge, is convinced that laughter and faith do not go together. Another, William of Baskerville, begs to differ. Their disagreement represents a fault line that has existed for centuries and still exists. Might laughter in church undermine the seriousness of God, the beauty of the liturgy and the sanctity of the Sacrament? If we began laughing, might we stop taking God seriously, let alone ourselves?

Baskerville is a follower of St Francis – the saint who was given to joy and merriment. At one point, St Francis preached a sermon to the birds, who apparently were much taken by it.[5] Jorge is not a great supporter of Franciscans – they are too light, too irreverent for him.

In the film[6] there is a memorable exchange between the two men. Jorge explains that he is disturbed by the Franciscans' openness to laughter. Baskerville acknowledges that St Francis had a funny bone. For Jorge there is something almost demonic about laughter – it is uncontrolled and makes men into something bestial. In one way he is right – there is something dangerous about laughter. But Baskerville points out that the animals actually never laugh so it

POLITICS, FOOLS AND SPEAKING   87

cannot make us like them. Indeed, it actually makes us like us.

Jorge then plays his trump card. He is not alone in playing it. He points out that Christ never laughed. It seems like he has the *coup de grace*. Baskerville waits awhile and then wonders aloud if we can be really sure that Christ never laughed. Jorge points out that there is nothing in Holy Scripture that says he did laugh (something that the great G.K. Chesterton had also realized). William Baskerville quietly points out that while there is no proof in Scripture that he did laugh, there is no proof either that he didn't.

The two discuss Aristotle's lost treatise on laughter. It is the book that Jorge has been trying to keep secret; he has poisoned the pages so those who thumb through in search of laughter end up dead. In the novel, the monastery has the only surviving copy.

William asks Jorge what is so alarming about laughter; why did he find it such a threat? Of course, it is the same threat that always confronts the powerful. Jorge explains that the church needs fear to keep people in line. Laughter is the great antidote to fear, it kills it stone dead. If fear has gone, then Jorge believes that faith will soon follow. Fear of the devil is needed because without it, there is no need for God. Laughter may be a way that fear of the devil – or anything else, for that matter – is swept away. In one sense, Jorge is onto something. He acknowledges the power of laughter. But in another, of course, he is a mile wide of the mark.

Baskerville knows that stopping laughter won't stop people trying to read Aristotle's book on humour and laughter. But that isn't really Jorge's deepest fear. His fear is this. He knows that ordinary people will always laugh. But what if clever and learned people said it was OK to laugh at anything? What if every aspect of life and love and existence were open to mirth? What if we found it all funny? Then we might get the idea that we could laugh at God.

We see here the great fear that if laughter and mirth escape, then perhaps the whole edifice of church might collapse. Can we laugh at God? It is a very good question. I certainly hope that we can at least laugh with him. In the form of Jesus, God seemed rarely to be on his dignity. And in the Old Testament the laughter of God seems limited to being aimed at the defeat of his enemies, or those who stand against him (e.g. Pss. 2:4; 37:13).

Laughter is often associated with mockery, which in the wrong hands can be very negative and destructive. But God 'mocks proud mockers', we are told in Proverbs 3:34. But where does this leave those who

Could mirth defeat the Nazis?

Hitler famously never told a joke. But could mirth be used as a weapon against him? The BBC certainly tested the theory, with interesting results. The BBC's German Service began in 1938 as an ad-hoc way of broadcasting Neville Chamberlain's 'peace' speech to the German people.[7]

When war broke out, it continued. It had an interesting dual strategy. The service reported the news and did so truthfully; it even reported British losses and defeats. This built up confidence in whatever else was broadcast. It points to the need for truth if we are to be taken seriously. Comedy is better when it comes from a truthful source.

> Comedy comes better when it is from a truthful source.

That 'whatever else' was satire – sketches painstakingly put together by a team of writers. The sketches concentrated on gently puncturing many of the Nazis' claims – especially that the war was going well for them. The satire also poked fun at the inconsistences of Hitler and his ideology.

It was clever – clever, because it made sure never to insult the German people and always to comment from small domestic scenarios that had the ring of truth. Characters were created: the chatty Berlin housewife, the gullible German corporal and the like. These were counterpointed by other characters that commented on their comments. It may have been propaganda, but it was also humour.

The German efforts were markedly different – rabid attacks on Britain, and Lord Haw-Haw's blatant, if sinister, exaggerations.

But did the BBC's efforts – it's mirthful counter-war – do any good? It is a moot point and one that was discussed at the BBC at the time. What was the point of entertaining the German people?

During the war there was a trickle of correspondence from listeners in Germany. Listening to the broadcast was punishable by death, so the small number is understandable. But after the war, a deluge of letters was received by the corporation. The writers thanked the BBC for keeping them alive. Some said they hated Hitler so much that they were wondering about committing suicide, but that the BBC broadcasts gave them hope in the future. The broadcasts gave many ordinary German people a sense of reality amid the madness of the Third Reich. The

POLITICS, FOOLS AND SPEAKING 91

broadcasts were a comfort and were appreciated – but was that a good enough reason for making the programmes?

So, we come back again to the mixed business of humour and politics and political change. Mirth is powerful. It is a sustainer and a vehicle of hope. The German listeners commented on the power of the sheer charm of the broadcasts. But did mirth cut even one day from the war? It was bombs and fighting and hunger perhaps that did that. It took the lives of many people and armies with guns and tanks to dislodge the evil of the Nazis. Indeed, comics can only now joke about the Establishment because the Establishment did all it could to give them the freedom to do so.

As we explore mirth, and especially its place in the faith and the church, we need to not expect too much from it. Or perhaps to expect a lot from it, but only in the places that it most works its magic and its healing.

Hitler never told jokes. Perhaps that is the one reason why we should.

But today?

Is there room to shake up the people and institutions of power? This might seem an odd question – satire is alive and well. Or is it? We live in a time when everyone's a critic – where social media bristles with indignations. The sheer volume of opinion and anger means that we have lost the power of the one voice – close to power, listened to by all.

There is no need for a court jester today because the court is surrounded and harried by them and so tends to block its ears. These days the reaction to biting, subtle, blunt or simply mad critique is to batten down the hatches and let the storm pass. Or to fight criticism with a dose of fake news. I despair for the fool, the court jester. I think that they have been opinioned out of existence, and for that I am sad.

But if speaking into power is a lost art, what about mirth as a way of speaking into our own experience? Or even: is mirth a way of holding up a mirror to the way that we are seen?

Study questions

I think that we might all agree that mirth (including humour) can be a good way of puncturing the delusions of the pompous – be that a person or institution.

In what way do we see the pompous and the powerful deflated by humour? What good does this kind of humour do?

The laughter in the hall was perhaps more prophetic than a signal of immediate change. The laughter was a comment on the world as it was and the preposterous notions that it lived out.

How can humour and mirth have a prophetic edge? How does humour comment on the ways of the world?

The German listeners commented on the power of the sheer charm of the broadcasts. But did mirth cut even one day from the war? It was bombs and fighting and hunger perhaps that did that. It took the lives of many people and armies with guns and tanks to dislodge the evil of the Nazis.

What kind of power does humour have? Does it have any political influence?

Prayer

Lord, bless those who are brave enough to speak up, using humour against vested interests. We pray that our society might listen to humourists and be prepared to change if we need to. We pray for those in places where humour and wit put them in danger. Let us not take ourselves too seriously.

9

Of Golf Courses and Helter-skelters

Changes afoot

The *Daily Mail* in 2018 reported[1] that our very senior clerics have a new spirit of boldness and adventure. The Archbishop of Canterbury said: 'If you can't have fun in a cathedral, do you really know what fun is?' It is a good point, although I had never actually associated cathedrals with fun – well not until now, anyway.

He made the comment after Sue Jones, the Dean of Liverpool, was criticized for organizing a Halloween service during which one of the cathedral hierarchy was wheeled into the cathedral in a coffin.

What a genius idea. I wonder why it is restricted to cathedrals. If cathedrals are loosening up to mirth and merriment, our other churches must be ripe for reinvention.

> If cathedrals are loosening up to mirth and merriment, our other churches must be ripe for reinvention.

Fairground cathedral

Actually, Rochester Cathedral must have one of the funniest and tongue-in-cheek straplines in the Church. Or at least I hope that it is tongue-in-cheek. The line is this: 'Growing in Christ since ad604'. My word, how much must they have grown in his likeness in all those years? They must be almost identical to him by now!

Perhaps it is because of this they have decided to invest in some good old-fashioned merriment. They set up a mini-golf course in the cathedral in 2019.[2] It probably isn't surprising that the move was divisive. The debate surrounding the golf is actually very interesting. It captures a certain mindset that sees holy places like cathedrals as frozen in time – sacred places where we need to be quiet. And make no mistake, I love places where I can be quiet.

The debate in general has been lively and I certainly don't want to trample over perfectly sensible objections.

People have complained that the golf course somehow made the church a place that is primarily about entertainment and not God. They have said it might make golfers rather than Christians. Some have called it a desecration of a holy space. Perhaps it is akin to inviting in the money lenders (Matt. 21:12), others have suggested. There has certainly been some holy outrage.[3]

I don't want to be overly critical of the negative voices. I certainly understand that setting up a McDonalds franchise in a cathedral, or a bouncy castle, might be a step too far for many. But if a cathedral has a shop, then it can also have a mini golf course. Even one called Fairway to Heaven. In my long years as an atheist, I think I would have valued the chance to go into a cathedral and be joyous and perhaps at that moment to wonder a little about God.

The golf/merriment experiment has had some interesting results which seem to argue against the negative voices. One sure-fire result is that more visitors came to the cathedral and its services. There are other examples of expanding the way we see and use cathedrals.

The move to jolly-up our cathedrals seems to have momentum. And each time the same objections are made – 'this kind of thing is beneath the dignity of the church'. But I argue that it is the 'dignity' of the church that has been, and is, the problem.

Norwich Cathedral installed a helter-skelter[4] – yes, a fairground helter-skelter – all 50ft-plus of it. Bringing the fairground into the cathedral was a beautifully bold move. The idea had a faith context, just like crazy golf in Rochester. The Rochester experiment had the bold insight that if you could just get people who don't usually come into a church, into a church, then they might find something about it that points them towards God.

Personally, I love the Norwich experiment and the Rochester one because they saw fun as a gift of the church and they offered it with no strings attached.

But I was disturbed by the level of opposition and the tone of it. The outrage seemed to come a little too easily. The objections appeared to arise from a place that wanted to preserve a church as a kind of museum-piece. So, I emailed the priest behind the Norwich merriment experiment – Canon Pastor Andy Bryant. I can do no better than replicate the email[5] because it explains the helter-skelter and much more. It explains the need for fun and playfulness – not as frivolity but as the very essence of life with God and each other.

Why did you set up the helter-skelter?

I wanted to help people get close to our wonderful medieval roof bosses – which are some of the best in the world. Not only are they beautifully carved, they also tell the story of the Bible. If I could get people closer to the bosses, my hope was that it would open up opportunities to share the Bible story. The helter-skelter was a playful way to achieve this serious ambition. I had originally wanted a ferris wheel but as they are all trailer-mounted, none could be moved into the cathedral. A helter-skelter comes in pieces and so could be built inside the cathedral. Although the helter-skelter was the headline event, there were a number of other installations all linked to the theme of 'Seeing it Differently'. Each day we also had fourteen trained volunteers mixing with visitors and open to encounters and conversations. The event was always missional in intention.

Challenges/opposition?

The few that objected were loud and often rude. Some reacted just to the helter-skelter and, when we explained the wider project then apologized. Clearly some people live with a lot of anger in them . . . I do get that at first sight for some the helter-skelter might be a provocative sight, but that is part of opening up the idea of 'Seeing it Differently', both by its presence in this space and the unique view it offered from the top. Overwhelmingly, however, the response has been favourable. Amongst those actually coming in to the cathedral, 99 per cent seemed in favour, with so many commenting on the atmosphere of joy and the presence of so many smiles.

What has it achieved?

There are so many wonderful stories and so many favourable comments. Each time I went into the cathedral someone would come up to me and shake my hand and say 'thank you'. All around me people were making friends with strangers. The most frequently used word was 'joy' . . .

Why is it a spiritual experience?

There were many faith conversations. Those new to the cathedral found themselves drawn to exploring the building further. Hundreds of copies of Gospels, books on prayer, leaflets on Christianity and other literature were given out. The candles lit and the prayers left saw a significant increase. Many stopped to read the stories of how Jesus had helped individuals see life differently. . . .

As Canon Pastor here, I take many serious and often heartbreaking services, but I also want to affirm that we were also made for love and laughter and fun. A church has to be a place where the whole of life is acknowledged and expressed, and that has to include fun.

In my ministry I have learned much from stand-up comics and buskers. They know how to work a crowd. With the large numbers queuing for this event, I too had to 'work the crowd', and laughter and fun in those conversations were vital and helped keep the atmosphere happy and relaxed.

Yes, this event was often playful, but always there was a serious intent. We smiled and we laughed but God was never forgotten, nor our desire to share the story. It is never either/or; God is present in both the tears and the laughter. And the wonderful thing about Norwich Cathedral is that it is big enough to contain a range of activities and a breadth of emotions all in the same moment.

At one end of the nave, a helter-skelter, at the [other] end of the nave, people lying still, looking up at the roof bosses. And at the east end in the stillness, people reading stories of how Jesus helps us see life differently, candles being lit and prayers offered. In these eleven days, the whole of life was known – surely that is being the true house of God.

Study questions

In my long years as an atheist, I think I would have valued the chance to go into a cathedral and be joyous and perhaps at that moment to wonder a little about God.

What do you make of this? How do you view cathedrals and other sacred places?

The Rochester experiment had the bold insight that if you could just get people who don't usually come into a church, into a church, then they might find something about it that points them towards God.

Do you think you might experience less of a sense of God in a church with a golf course in it?

As Canon Pastor here, I take many serious and often heartbreaking services, but I also want to affirm that we were also made for love and laughter and fun. A church has to be a place where the whole of life is acknowledged and expressed, and that has to include fun.

Do you agree? In what way can a church be a place of fun, and what might this say about God?

Prayer

Thank you for the initiatives that encourage mirth and connection with you. Help us to be open-minded and to be gracious with those who differ from us. Lord, we wonder what it might be like if we opened our churches to a sense of play and fun and encouraged visitors to also experience you in this.

10

The Unintentional Merriment and Mirth of Church

At the end of the service, one of my congregation called me over. I didn't recognize them, they were new. In fact, it was the one and only time I saw them at church.

Person
Vicar, do you actually prepare your sermons? You know, write them down?

Me [Hurt]
Yes. Why? (I'm not someone who dashes off a sermon at the last moment. I take care.)

Person [Cheerful]
Can I take it home with me?

Me [Encouraged]
Good. Do you want to read it again? We can meet and discuss it?

Person
No, it's not that. I fell asleep as you started speaking, and only woke up when you said amen. I wanted to see what you said.

There was much to be admired about this person. Their honesty and directness were refreshing, and yes, we can sometimes drone on with our sermons.

I wonder whether, if we celebrated this kind of humorous interaction, we might begin to see church as a place where we had a smile on our faces. Church is a place of frequent unintended comedy. But what if, too, it was a place where our exuberance and acceptance of God's love created a space where mirth was as natural as seriousness?

At the heart of church as a crucible of comedy is the issue of dissonance. Ordinary people collide with a holy place and the results are often funny. One imagines that in times past when church was more a part of people's lives, the dissonance may not have

THE UNINTENTIONAL MERRIMENT 107

been so great. But these days going to church is like visiting a foreign land without a guidebook. Or perhaps the dissonance is as old as the hills. Whenever a holy God is in contact with time-bound and earthy humans, then it is ripe for misunderstanding, slapstick and observational comedy.

We humans are a bunch of contradictions. We are matter, but we also have something soulful about us. We are full of high ideals, sacrifice and purpose, and yet we are also infected with selfishness, pride and all manner of sins. We want to do one thing, but we do the other.[1] And when you add all this up and herd people into church for a service that involves reading, praying, singing and standing up and sitting down, then we are in the holy ground of mirth. Add into that the intrinsically comedic character of 'the vicar' and who knows where it might lead?

There are many other good reasons why church is a place of unintended comedy. I want to say it's because the Holy Spirit is around and he has a way of helping us to see the funny side of things. I love to think that one of the fruits of being born again (John 3:3) is a propensity to light-heartedness, jollity and fun.

But there are also structural reasons why Church and unintentional comedy are such good partners.

When people come to church, they are so often on their best behaviour, and that is a recipe for disaster. If we aren't feeling natural, then frequently, we aren't acting natural. People often feel they have to clean up their act – especially when faced with a person wearing a dog collar.

Someone quite new to the church was doing the reading on a Sunday. As the person got up, I noticed how nervous they looked. I smiled in order to help them relax. But my family tell me that my smile is frequently unnerving. And so it proved.

The person was about to begin when they looked over at me, imploringly.

'Sorry vicar, I left my glasses back in the pew.'

I smiled magnanimously. The glasses were retrieved. But as the person was about to begin reading, they knocked the Bible off the lectern onto the floor and uttered a loud expletive.

Looking full of embarrassment, they picked up the Bible and started leafing frantically through it. After a few seconds he semi-shouted the name of the Lord, which of course I took as a prayer. But it is a good example of the flummoxing that happens when we feel we are in an alien environment and

THE UNINTENTIONAL MERRIMENT 109

out of our depth. It also says to me why I want to try to avoid people feeling this way in church. I go out of my way to celebrate failures like this, and our congregation rises – or should that be falls – magnificently to the occasion.

In this case they laughed along and gave a round of applause. This certainly helped because the person wasn't put off from reading during a service again. Our clumsy reader was in fact in a direct line of descent from Christ's friends and followers who frequently said and did the wrong things and got mixed up.

Another reason why church is such a good incubator for unintentional comedy is that the people we attract are so varied. There is no other institution like church anywhere in our society. Anyone can join. People can come when they like. We don't check their credentials, or their views or theology. It is open house. Perhaps the only analogy is the great British pub.

When you put together a collection of people as varied as those who turn up to church, then there is bound to be comedy. I despair at churches that draw their clientele from a narrow band. In those churches, I feel as though I am in an echo chamber with people with similar ideas and backgrounds. I long for the beautiful chaos of the local church. I understand the impulse that says 'let us specialize and offer something targeted at a certain group'; of course I do: I worked in marketing before I became a priest.

But for me, the parish church is the purest form of church because of its diversity, and that diversity helps comedy take centre stage. We find each other funny – we aren't all thinking or acting the same way. This sense of people from wildly different backgrounds all in one place worshipping the invisible God has been eat and drink for the sitcom writers.

> But for me, the parish church is the purest form of church because of its diversity.

There's also the point that, by and large, we are a volunteer organization. It is true that some churches are very slick and have an army of paid workers – all experts in certain fields. There is nothing wrong with this. Indeed, it is a great and beautiful thing to behold. I don't buy the charge of creeping managerialism in the church at all.

But in my little church in north London, I am the only full-time paid person. All the other roles are made up of people who have volunteered, and that can cause beautiful havoc at times. We have to have

THE UNINTENTIONAL MERRIMENT 111

the square peg in the round hole because that is the only peg we have. It sometimes feels like *Dad's Army*. But viewed with kindness rather than impatience, the mess-ups and good intentions fill me with warmth and a sense that it is good to be alive. And here there is an important point. Never trust a priest who is too uptight and controlling. 'Go with the flow' should be taught at all theological colleges.

A friend tells me that she put together a party to tidy up a chaotic room in a church outbuilding. It was cobwebbed and hadn't been visited for years. She appointed a small team to throw things away.

My friend came across a pile of very old newspapers.

'Great, let's chuck these,' she said.

'We can't throw them, they belong to Ed,' one of the specialist team answered.

'I'll speak to Ed, he won't mind,' said the vicar.

'You can't speak to him.'

'Why?'

'He's been dead for three years.'

Peter opens mouth and inserts foot

Interestingly, there is a very modern moment in the New Testament where one of Jesus' followers acts just like many people do in the modern church. Peter, who goes on to lead the early church, gets himself in a muddle. He is like a rabbit caught in the headlights, wrestling for the right thing to say and do. We see the incident in Matthew's Gospel.

Jesus takes his chosen few potential leaders up a high mountain. It's just Peter, James and John and him. I wonder if Peter felt a bit nervous. Perhaps he wanted to shine. Maybe he just didn't want to make a fool of himself. But on such sentiments, catastrophe can piggyback. None of the three disciples could have been expecting what happened next.

Jesus is transfigured before them. We are told that Jesus' face 'shone like the sun, and his clothes became as white as the light' (Matt. 17:2).

But just as it got startling, something even odder and more magnificent happens. The followers realize that Moses and Elijah – the heroes of Israel and both long dead – have turned up and are talking to Jesus.

The best, and perhaps only, tactic for Peter and his friends was surely to stay silent. What could anyone

THE UNINTENTIONAL MERRIMENT

say? But dear old Peter blunders in. Even 2,000 years distant, the unintentional humour of the moment is still painful.

> Peter said to Jesus, 'Lord, it is good for us to be here. If you wish, I will put up three shelters – one for you, one for Moses and one for Elijah.'
> *Matthew 17:4*

You can almost see the tumbleweed blowing across the set. It is a silly suggestion. It is a gaffe brought on by nerves and keenness and feeling a bit out of his depth. Thankfully, God the Father makes an appearance and covers the scene in a cloud which both announces his appearance and covers up Peter's embarrassment; although they also realize that the Jesus who is their friend is also nothing less than the Son of God.

There is an interesting end to this incident, and it is one that we who yearn for more mirth and merriment in our church would do well to heed. The followers are at this stage on the ground face-planted. They are terrified. We underestimate also how terrifying being in church can be, with all that standing up and sitting down and hymns we don't know and odd words we say that are in bold in the booklet. Going to a full-on charismatic service with hand-raising and loud music can also be scary to people who know nothing about church.

If we want mirth and merriment, and I think that most of us do, we need to do something to make church feel like home – a place you can truly be yourself in. The unintentional comedy of church is good for an anecdote. It keeps many a clergy dinner party going and is a welcome relief from the rigours of funerals and despair that many of us encounter. I celebrate the silliness that happens in church, and long may that continue.

But this can only be transformed into something beautiful if we behave with gentleness and lightness to those around us. Look what happens after the transfiguration fiasco.

> But Jesus came and touched them. 'Get up,' he said. 'Don't be afraid.' When they looked up, they saw no one except Jesus.
>
> *Matthew 17:7,8*

It would have been so easy for God-among-us to be cross with Peter. He could have scolded him or given him the cold shoulder. He could have decided that he was no longer leadership material. He could have been cross with all three followers, wondering why two of them sat looking like frightened schoolboys.

But he took them onto that mountain for a reason. In part, it was so they could see the glory of their leader – to know some truths. They see him now as in the line of Elijah and Moses, the great liberators of the people of God. They know now that he is a being of power beyond the human imagination. But that is only part of the education and, dare I say, not the most important part to me. There is something we all need to learn, and it is part of being a fully fledged grown-up, and that is to see perfectionism for the curse that it can be.

Jesus schooled them that making mistakes is OK. He showed them that he had a sense of humour, perhaps. I wonder if he smiled when he realized what a tizzy his friend was getting himself into. I wonder if it made him feel even closer to his mate Peter – the tough fisherman who wanted to be liked and frequently put his foot in it.

What he does is touch them – perhaps puts his hand in theirs and helps them to their feet. 'Don't be afraid, my friends,' is his call. Why? Because fear is the opposite of love, and if we can stop being *afraid* of God (rather than being in awe of him, a 'holy fear' or respect), or anyone else for that matter, then we can be free to be people of jollity and mirth and merriment. And people like that truly live out what it is to be fully alive.

As church we can reach out and help people not to be afraid – not afraid to be eccentric, or quiet, or jolly, or thoughtful.

Of communion and cats

At my church, before Covid-19 interrupted our lives, we had a communion service each week on a Thursday. We got about eight people – our regulars. At one point in the service, we had a short discussion of the Bible passage for the day. On one particular week, I was discussing a psalm that praised the beauty and wonder of the natural world – the birds, fish and animals. I pointed out that if we wrote Psalm 8 today, we might include pets.

There was much nodding and agreement. Then one of my regulars piped up with a comment so random that we had to pause for a collective laugh. This is what she said: 'Ah, I have a pet cat, vicar. Have you ever seen those photos where they take pictures from underneath a cat while it's sitting on a glass table?'

As one we said, 'No.'

She fished out her phone, tapped out a web address and showed us the picture of a cat from beneath.

'Look,' she said. 'You can see its huge, hairy buttocks.'

What if unintended comedy has more to offer?

What if this rich and beautiful vein of comedy isn't a sideshow – what if it is a signal to something much more profound? What if this kind of caper is actually our greatest selling point as a church; if we treasured and celebrated it – even encouraged it – might the church be so rammed with people that we'd have to put in a second storey?

I know that the church has become very adept at doing slickness. Some of the events are now called 'conferences' and they feel like an A-grade business conference. Many churches have professional musicians and many preachers travel the world with a well-worked hour's talk to deliver. There is nothing at all wrong here, and I love to be part of this kind of thing – sometimes. But not every week, and not in my chosen place of worship; I might be tempted to feel a bit superior, or even to fall in love with a worldliness that I want to speak up against.

The church, with its amateurism, jumble sales and wobbly chairs and people, might seem like an anachronism. But perhaps we are the antidote to all that is shiny and professional. Perhaps the comedy is what helps people to bring the humour of their own lives into the presence of God. Perhaps it is the kind of silliness and comedy value of church that chimes well with our picture of the 'foolishness of God' (1 Cor. 1:25).

Which brings me back to Jesus – the homespun God. Christ is in anguish, near-terror. He is about to go into Jerusalem to face the most agonizing death. He knows what awaits him. It isn't just the torture. It is the taking onto himself of every bad thing that ever happened. I try not to forget that he was going to need the help of an angel to minister to him just to get him to the cross (Luke 22:43).

Around the time of Christ's entering into Jerusalem, a grand and slick parade is entering Jerusalem by another gate. The Roman legion was on its way, and it was a great spectator event – indeed, everyone who was anyone would have been thrusting not just to look but to be seen there.[2]

It would have been full of pomp and ceremony and might. It would have been choreographed. Christ, on the other hand, is not arriving on a chariot flanked by soldiers in uniform. He is coming on a donkey and is being cheered along by a rag-tag bunch of people who presumably couldn't be bothered to make

THE UNINTENTIONAL MERRIMENT

the 'real' parade. They were waving palm fronds (Matt. 21:5–9). Yes, there is a symbolism of kingship attached to the donkey (Zech. 9:9). But it has a comedy about it that is based on something or someone grand being suddenly thrust onto something that is humble and shambling. It is as though Christ was more comfortable with something much less slick than a chariot. Of course, he could have entered Jerusalem flanked by thousands of angels if he had wanted to.

I wonder what kind of church Christ might pop into if he were living here now. Where he might unobtrusively slip in at the back . . . Would it be the grandeur and perfection of, say, Rome? Or might he feel more at home in a church that seemed to be incapable of getting everything right?

The unintended comedy of church might be our greatest glory because it speaks of our weakness and not our strengths. Perhaps, 'blessed are the clumsy and the silly and the plain daft'?

Study questions

I love to think that one of the fruits of being born again . . . is a propensity to light-heartedness, jollity and fun.

What do you make of this?

Peter, who goes on to lead the early church, gets himself in a muddle. He is like a rabbit caught in the headlights, wrestling for the right thing to say and do.

Can you think of examples of unintentional humour in church, or any formal setting?

What he does is touch them – perhaps puts his hand in theirs and helps them to their feet. 'Don't be afraid my friends,' is his call. Why? Because fear is the opposite of love, and if we can stop being afraid of God . . . or anyone else for that matter, then we can be free to be people of jollity and mirth and merriment.

What do you think of Jesus' gesture? How would it have made you feel? How might you do this kind of thing to reassure others?

Prayer

Thank you for the mess-ups and mistakes that make church so entertaining and keep us amused. Help us to not take each other too seriously and to cut other people some slack. Thank you that Peter made such spectacular mistakes and for the way we can take comfort from them. Help us to reassure people who make mistakes as well. Help us to celebrate them.

11

The Comedy Vicar

Eccentrics, the *bon viveur*, and rogues

If you fancy a laugh, I most merrily recommend the Reverend Fergus Butler-Gallie's modern classic, *A Field Guide to the English Clergy*.[1] With tongue firmly pressed into cheek, Butler-Gallie presents a rogue's gallery of wayward clergy – all Anglican, all men and all dead.

There is something very pleasing about this unholy mob – not least the sense of devil-may-care in our modern age of taking things very seriously. It has something of the Carry On film about it. It is odd the way these rogues cheer us up.

Butler-Gallie has some interesting points to make. He argues that a combination of eccentricity and Englishness is a potent cocktail for mirth and comedy. The eccentricity that still runs through national life is mirrored and exaggerated by the fact that vicars themselves are so often eccentric. This is why the stereotype of the comedy vicar is so close to our secular nation's heart. Vicars have something of the clown about them. It comes with the job and the kind of people who are attracted to holy orders.

He also argues that there is something of the inbuilt merriment of the *bon viveur* about many vicars. It is hard to disagree. When I left theological college, our principal told us very solemnly that we should not be the first to get to the table of food, or the last one to leave the bar. It is good advice, but I fear it may have fallen on deaf ears.

The early model

The vicar has long been a staple of British novels and television. Indeed, one of the very earliest novels, *The Life and Opinions of Tristram Shandy*,

Gentleman[2] featured a certain Pastor Yorick, who created a template for the comedy vicar for many centuries to come.

Parson Yorick is nice. He is a little unworldly and he is patient. He alone is prepared to sit and listen to the novel's eponymous hero as he talks and talks and talks. What makes Yorick all the more interesting is that he is a thinly veiled picture of the novelist himself. Laurence Sterne, the author, was a vicar.

The novel was a sensation. It both lit up the literary world and established a new genre as the novel began to get established as a new artform. The book is a sprawling comic masterpiece.

But we have to see it, and the comic vicar, in context.[3] The comic vicar is a part of British literary life, and later, TV life. Some things have remained constant. Largely, the vicar has been a figure of affection. Largely, too, the vicar is portrayed as unworldly, although benign. The ways of the world have been a rich source of comic confusion in the lives of vicars. But there have been subtle changes, and it is these which have got us to a state where the vicar may be comic, but they are also largely irrelevant.

> The comic vicar is a part of British literary life, and later, TV life.

THE COMEDY VICAR

At the birth of the novel in the eighteenth century, Sterne set the pattern for the portrayal for vicars. His pastor is kind, a good man and in no way a figure of fear. But while those early vicars may have been unworldly, they were also robust. They weren't pathetic. They had backbone. Parson Adams in Henry Fielding's novel *Joseph Andrews*[4] is prepared to stick up for himself.

Victorian fiction is full of vicars. It is no surprise, as the church was perhaps the major employer of influential middle-class men at the time. In the Victorian novel, the clergyman is not absurd as a matter of course. They are good, solid people battling with the challenges of Darwinism and what it is to have faith.

But if we scroll forward, what then? What of the vicar in a world that has lost connection with theology, and where religion is at the very least a minority pastime? Perhaps the only place for the comic vicar to go is to one where they are just comic. We shall see.

British TV vicars

What are we to make of the strange case of TV vicars? In the 1970s we had Dick Emery's easily shocked vicar. To capture the mood, Emery wore a set of outsize teeth.

Perhaps the most loved portrayal of a vicar was Dawn French's Geraldine Granger in *The Vicar of Dibley*. But what can we learn from the way it depicts the vicar as a comedy character, and can our quest for mirth and merriment find a place of nourishment here?

The humour works on a number of levels. Perhaps it is most realistic in realizing that the authentic humour to be had is as much with the congregation as the vicar herself. Dibley serves up a delightful assortment of odd characters, all of whom are looking for something slightly different from the vicar. It is touching the way the vicar's congregation rely on her and it is hilarious that they are needy, odd, rude, ribald and thoroughly themselves.

But when we press into the vicar herself, we don't find ourselves on such strong ground. Some of the humour is self-deprecating. Granger makes fun of her weight and her looks.

At other turns we see the clash between rural conservatism and the church and Granger's liberal city ways. It is a sitcom staple as old as the genre itself. Another of these established tropes is the fish-out-of-water syndrome. Granger isn't used to country ways and she finds it hard to settle in, and much merriment ensues.

THE COMEDY VICAR

The programme pokes gentle fun at the Church of England – which is, of course, perfectly fine.

So, why do I have my doubts? Well, the TV vicar and the vicar of the novels do no harm. Indeed, they might humanize a church that is elsewhere often portrayed as angular and spiky and hard-to-like. The TV vicar is a national treasure.

But my problem is, and this is taking Dibley as a model to stand in for all TV vicars, that the comic portrayal of the British vicar only tells a very small part of the story. In some ways, the portrayal tames the vicar and forces them into a role. It is very much the way the Christ is tamed into the role of gentle and mild holder of lambs – and not the fiery God who made the universe.

The comedy vicar shows how comedy itself can neutralize something that is wilder and transformative. As we laugh at Granger, we are laughing at a made-for-TV vicar – the kind that is acceptable: sassy, liberal and trendy. But in my experience, vicars have much more to offer than this airbrushed jokefest.

Indeed, by domesticating the vicar in a cloak of silliness, we lose the light and shade of the life of vicars and the dark, dark humour and mirth that we live through.

The vicars I know love a joke and are funny. They are also wise and know the battles people face. We are with people as they face existential crises, lose loved ones and face death and destruction. We are with them at their marriages and the baptism of children. We sit with them in their homes and have a cup of tea and listen to the stories of their lives. We preach the good news even when we feel empty inside. And sometimes we see their lives and our lives transformed by the gentle and beautiful presence of God. Some weeks we feel lonely and other times we feel sprightly and full of hope – just like everyone else.

In this rich tapestry of being a priest, there is scope for a different kind of merriment and mirth and humour that isn't a sitcom.

Even in the darkest moments there are tender shards of mirth. When all looks lost in a person's life, I often hear them say something touching, or funny, or self-knowing.

Back in 2010 the BBC tried to reflect something of this reality in *Rev.*, written by Tom Hollander and James Wood. It features an inner-city vicar, Adam Smallbone, played by Hollander. The dynamics of inner-city life, a wife who is a reluctant clergy spouse and the usual array of stock weird parishioners flesh out the rest. But there is a problem. The name given to the vicar signals something of his impotence.

In some ways Revd Smallbone is the perfect very modern TV vicar. He is no longer really a one-dimensional figure of fun. Instead, he is just clinging on – as the faith is. The show is low on laughs, but much modern comedy is. In some ways he feels like the emblem of despair. He is certainly a long way from the robust Parson Adams.

It isn't that *Rev.* hasn't some truth and poignant moments. But it misses the chance of showing the real mirth at the heart of ministry. It misses the passion of the gospel. The only time an ounce of oompf is injected is when a new curate arrives – straight from an evangelical church. The world-weary Smallbone is seen as a virtuous counterpoint to her enthusiasm and earnestness. Smallbone isn't going anywhere in the church. He is raggedy and unglamorous. It all feels like the end for the comedy vicar.

The weight of humour

You may well say that I am loading too much weight onto mirth and merriment and its cousin, humour. You may be right. But if I expect that mirth and merriment are the last-forgotten verities of the church, then we have to expect a bit more.

I wonder what a comedy vicar created by a Christian might actually look like? One of the problems is that so many of the TV representations are written at a distance from the real thing.

I think there is something intrinsically mirthful and funny and merry about being a vicar. I am a vicar in the London borough of Brent, in one of the most ethnically diverse places on the planet. Each week I find things that fill me with joy. Things make me laugh. Sometimes its mistakes we make. Sometimes our guests. I love the discomfiture of someone issuing an expletive or using fruity language and then saying, 'Oh, sorry vicar,' as though I've never used that language myself. I'm from Northolt. My dad was an East End carpet fitter.

At our memory café we have joyful times even in the face of dementia — which is the devil's own illness. We do it because we can and because we trust that dementia isn't the end of the story of our lives. I can truly say that I have had more fun at memory café — singing old songs, sharing a joke, listening to life stories — than I've ever had down the pub or at a comedy show. It is a deep merriment born of community spirit, shared lives and old songs. It is centred by beautiful food provided free-of-charge by a local Sikh charity. It is blessed with a choir where the only qualification you need is to be still breathing.

Our café is merriment personified and lived-out fifty-one weeks of the year – although, of course, the coronavirus pandemic has interrupted us. It is merriment in the very face of the pain and suffering we go through. I call it an unexpected explosion of joy. That's what being a vicar is about. That's what I think the depiction of vicars misses.

All of this is made sharper and more absurd by the fact that the Church of England is part of the tapestry of national life. Perhaps the endearing comedy vicar is here still, because the country demands it. The Church of England, in which I am a priest, is still part of our country's landscape. (It is interesting that we haven't ever had a comedy free-church pastor!)

The Brits tend to find humour in all the staples – the weather, the food, queuing. So, of course, the comedy vicar has to line up and take their place. The comedy vicar is as inevitable as the red bus and the post box.

Study questions

The eccentricity that still runs through national life is mirrored and exaggerated by the fact that vicars themselves are so often eccentric. This is why the stereotype of the comedy vicar is so close to our secular nation's heart.

Does this ring true? Why do you think the comedy vicar still has a place in the nation's heart?

Indeed, by domesticating the vicar in a cloak of silliness, we lose the light and shade of the life of vicars and the dark, dark humour and mirth that we live through.

Do you think that comedy vicars stop us from seeing the 'real' comedy of the vocation?

I wonder what a comedy vicar created by a Christian might actually look like?

Well – what do you think?

Prayer

Thank you for the inherent comedy in the vicar's vocation. Long may it continue, and may the vicar remain a figure of endearment. But Lord, help us to show the other strands of the dark comedy of the vicar.

12

Stand-up and Be Counted

What happens if we dissect humour, analyse it or put it under the microscope? Will it survive? Might it die on the dissecting table? Will it help us to understand why we need it so much and why we convulse our bodies in laughter when we are exposed to it? Is laughter a way of confronting our pain and emptiness?

Research

I did some extensive field research on mirth, merriment and comedy. It took the form of two weeks at the Edinburgh Fringe in 2019 – the world's biggest and best arts and comedy festival. It was a truly mind-boggling experience, with simply thousands of shows each week. The streets were packed with people handing out flyers.

It is, perhaps, the most perfect comedy and theatre market in the world, based on a strong ethic of survival of the fittest. I am sure that most shows make a loss – there is simply a huge oversupply issue. Shows live or die as the performers strive to get their voice heard in an incredibly noisy environment.

But as the fourteen days moved on, I came to admire more and more the creativity and effort that had gone into all these shows. From the show with a handful of visitors to the 3,000-seater events, the Fringe is a kind of hymn to mirth and merriment, and we would do well to listen to what it is whispering to us.

It is easy to do church in a bubble. It is equally easy to demonize the world of comedy, and there is some very dark stuff indeed out there. Often the language is appalling and the subject matter, to say the very least, ill-judged. But the shape and structure of so many of the shows highlight the extraordinary power of the arts to speak into our lives and to teach us while at the same time helping us to laugh, or perhaps just give a gentle smile.

So, what can we learn on our quest for the church and Christian community with mirth and merriment at its heart? What is Edinburgh teaching us? At the very least, the Fringe is vastly popular, drawing millions of people from around the world (pre-Covid!), so it has to have something. But it is also a vision of what things might be like if artists ruled the world.

Improv

Those of a certain vintage will remember the hit Channel 4 show, *Whose Line Is It Anyway?* It announced the skills of improv to an unsuspecting British public. Improv continued to be very popular. On the night I popped in to see some of the original TV cast doing *Whose Line . . .* at the Fringe, the place was packed.

Although the cast may have lacked some of the original vigour, it was hard not to be impressed by their craft of improv. You could see the way the participants were able to take one idea and quickly morph it into a string of connections. They needed to be alive to what the others were doing and go with the flow. The improv worked well when something unexpected happened and what seemed like an ordinary suggestion became gloriously silly.

STAND-UP AND BE COUNTED 137

In some ways the charismatic movement has allowed the church be more open to the skills of improv, although they would probably say that they take their cue from that great improviser, the Holy Spirit. The movement has helped to free up the church to the possibilities of newness and spontaneity. It has reminded us of the vibrancy of the Holy Spirit.

But something says to me that this is only part of the picture. I worry that the charismatic experience of 'improv' is largely a personalized experience. Where secular improv is so wonderful is that it involves everyone all at the same time and with the same visual stimulus. And, of course, improv is beautifully silly and funny, which at least for me, hasn't been my 'charismatic' experience. There is an odd seriousness in the charismatic expressions and, for some, a feeling of guilt if they don't quite feel it like last time.

Improv is liberating because there isn't that kind of pressure. But improv is an interesting mirth model. The mirthful church might benefit from more improv, but that doesn't mean ditching all rules.

What you notice about professional improv troupes is that there are rules and there are ways of being. The ebb and flow of improv is choreographed – if it wasn't, it wouldn't be funny. Chaos generally isn't much fun. Even in a more liturgical church, improvised minutes of silence can be powerful. And a priest who knows when to break the third wall and say something funny and pertinent can be equally powerful. There are times to break rules.

The funniest of Jesus' miracles, found in John 2, is surely the first. He is at the wedding of a young couple. They run out of wine, which is a disaster on a number of fronts. Perhaps the main disaster is breaching the etiquette of hospitality. If the guests were to realize the wine had run out, they would never live it down. It would blight them and their marriage.

It is time for a bit of improvisation – and a cheeky bit at that. Prompted by his dear mother, Jesus decides on the hoof to make sure the guests do not run out of wine. He can't go to the local off licence, and so he decides to make some wine himself, and not just any wine – the most delicious wine imaginable. Presumably just the kind of wine people wouldn't expect at the young couple's wedding.

I imagine Christ looking round – he needs a prop or something to carry out the winemaking. All that is available are the large pots holding the purified and blessed water for cleansing the guests. This would render the guests ceremonially clean and was essential for the demands of piety and decency. The water has been blessed by the requisite religious leader.

'Perfect,' thinks Christ. 'I will use this sacred water and turn it into something that may not be sacred but that is needed to save the couple's blushes and create the best party in living memory.'

It is a scandal. It is full of naughtiness. It is funny, and it is a good example of ancient improv. One can almost hear the MC giving the improv actors the task – using the sacred water do something that brings the party to life.

I want to be a vicar who understands the improv craft, because without it, any mirth we generate and cherish has the potential to be stilted and pre-planned.

Mime and communicating without words

One of the highlights of my Fringe visit was a French mime show. I know it's a patently obvious thing to say, but it amazed me how close one could feel to characters on stage when they have not said a word. By the end of the show, I really felt that I knew the characters and I cared about what happened to them.

I am very much a words person. I love to write. I value words, and it goes back to my early days growing up. My mother would always push me to enlarge my vocabulary. I have a sense that we are what we say. If we don't have a word for something, how can we be sure that it exists?

But my time at the mime show made me wonder about the value of communicating without words. Plus, of course, the show was deeply funny. With the words cleared out, the mirth had room to mature and speak for itself.

I wonder if we might use gesture more often in church; if we also might embrace the power of communicating without words.

There is one striking moment in the New Testament where Jesus communicated through gesture, and it is especially poignant.

He is in a difficult situation. A woman caught in adultery is brought to him (John 8:1–11). What shall be done with her? The standard punishment is death – the only punishment, in fact. Christ does an odd thing. He crouches down and refrains from saying anything. Instead, he makes a mark in the sand.

We can imagine the pause – the silence. It is as though eternity holds its breath. What kind of savage judgement will follow and what violence? But the woman is not condemned to the death penalty. Instead, he uses this moment's pause to begin the process of helping the on-looking men to think about their own behaviour.

We don't get a sense of the Christ's gestures very often. We don't know how he used movement. But I hope that he made people laugh just by a flick of the hand or a move of the face and body. I sometimes imagine that he might have winked, or smiled, or acted out a funny movement.

And I wonder if, as a preacher, I might sometimes stop the babble of words and sometimes use gesture and silence.

Interestingly, Christ's crucifixion operated mainly without words. It is an acted-out symbol, a mime of despair and hopelessness turned to hope and joy.

Story-telling, anecdotes and song

It was the alternative comedy of the 1980s that began to thrust a different comedy upon us. That comedy largely did away with jokes and started the path to comics telling anecdotes. The comedy was acted out with funny stories and observations. It was a way of people showing how they saw the world and related to it. This was quite different to the mother-in-law jokes of the 1970s.

Edinburgh 2019 was a feat of anecdotal humour. Some shows were one-hour monologues – stories of an event or events. Others were a splicing together of different stories and perhaps songs. The narrative comedian is alive and well.

What makes this kind of comedy so interesting is that it is frequently non-linear. It is prepared to stop and look at something and move on long before the subject is exhausted.

It is so familiar that we forget that this kind of thing is relatively new. But it plays perfectly to the modern mindset and world view. We have a mistrust of big, overarching narratives. But we understand that everyone has a story and that story can be laced with humour and mirth. We see a comedian tell their story and we laugh along as we realize that we have had similar incidents and insights.

The comedy of anecdote and well-picked example is the modern comedy. It is also the ancient comedy of Jesus. He relates stories of his everyday life and the life of the people around him. You can imagine the murmurs of recognition as he tells a story.

STAND-UP AND BE COUNTED

This is certainly one area where modern preachers tend to excel. I have rarely heard a modern sermon without anecdote. Modern talks aim to engage people and make links. But all may not be well.

Comedy tends to take risks with anecdotes. It often stretches an anecdote beyond where we might think it would go. Am I alone in finding so much modern preaching a bit hackneyed and safe? I want to hear the real stories of our pastors and their wrestling with faith. The details of when their best-laid plans went wrong and refused to go right. I don't want to hear stories that are about funny family events all the time.

> Comedy tends to take risks with anecdotes.

The comedy of anecdote is risky.

Of course, I hate the kind of sermon that tells people off but lets the preacher go scot-free. I dislike the 'confessional' sermon that mentions some tiny wrong and then invites the listeners to confess really chunky misdemeanours.

Sight gags and silliness

I am a sucker for silliness and sight gags. That year at Edinburgh my favourite comic was a master of the art of being silly. Battery-powered teeth, puppets and odd inventions created a comedy that was rather beautiful. The sillier it got, the more I didn't want it to end.

This show also used some new technology. A loop pedal[1] allowed the comedian to make up songs on the spot and various instruments completed the odd sense of being in a parallel universe.

The strange thing about it was that the sheer innocence of the piece was most moving. It was as though we had been transported back to childhood for an hour. But the sight gags also allowed the comedian to comment on his tangled domestic life, the way he loved his kids and his struggles with writing comedy. Silliness and seriousness were actually quite comfortable together.

I have heard jokes from the front at church. Sadly, these have been pretty awful. But I don't think I have ever seen deliberate and beautiful silliness. I heard a story once about St Francis. I have never been able to track it down so I can't verify it, but I'm sure he won't mind me attributing it to him.

Francis is booked to give a sermon at an important service in an important church. He walks to the front and into the pulpit. He stands in silence for what seems like a long time. He then opens and closes his mouth without a sound coming out. After a few minutes of this he simply says, 'Amen.'

He had no words. He wasn't able to come up with a sermon. All he had was 'Amen' to the difficulty of saying anything about God.

I wonder if we encouraged more silliness we might capture some intrinsic truth about the 'silliness' of God. The God who puts 'the last first' (Mark 10:31) uses the most hopeless people for his work and recruits a set of disciples who act like Keystone Cops.

Jokes

What are we to do about jokes? I have certainly heard plenty of lame ones on a Sunday morning. It's tempting to ask for a ban on them on the grounds of crimes against comedy.

But we live in a time when to joke at all is dangerous. There are many just and reasonable sensitivities around. Perhaps the difficulty of telling jokes has led to more comedy of different types – character comedy, for instance.

Character comedy

This works by inhabiting another character and seeing life through their lens. Character comedy allows for flights of fancy. It allows us to comment and to see what it feels like to be someone else.

We sometimes forget when reading the Bible that we are dealing with characters and not simply truth. The temptation is to mine the Scripture for what it means and for what it means for us, rather than simply letting it work as a story and to inhabit the lives of the characters in that story.

So, when Jesus spots a reviled tax collector up a tree (Luke 19:1–10), we might wonder what that tax collector thought about the enquiry to let Jesus come for dinner. How was he feeling? How did it fit into the story of his life? We can similarly enter into the characters of all the actors on all the stages we find in the Bible.

This isn't just a flight of fancy. It helps us to see the Bible as something that lives and breathes and is the authentic story of real people and families. When we see the characters as having depth, we begin to apply some of our own challenges and perspectives to the story, and we can be less fraught about having to understand exactly what everything means.

Even when we read the letters of St Paul, we can begin to unpick the characters at work. And if we enter into the struggles of Paul, we can perhaps see a character beset by depression and perfectionism who struggles at times to overcome his character flaws – just like the rest of us.

The dark side

It would be easy to simply say that the Fringe has it all! But that year alone I heard many things that troubled me. There were jokes about self-harm and rape and paedophilia. Some might say that nothing should be beyond the reach of humour. But I disagree. Shock-tactic comedy is lazy. Just saying a shocking word will generally get a response. The same with a shocking subject.

I am glad that we are generally more sensitive about humour. I don't see it as the march of a stultifying political correctness. But as I sat watching various comedians, I realized that jokes about certain subjects aren't funny or needed. They aren't life-enhancing in any way. Interestingly, no comedian at the Fringe would tell a fat-shaming joke, or a racist one. So, where do we draw the line?

Jesus was regularly offensive. It was part of his ministry. He met with the kind of people the religious authorities thought were not to be mixed with. It seems sometimes that he went out of his way to be offensive (see for example Matt. 15:26). In the Bible there are references to all kinds of bodily fluids and earthy situations. The NIV has St Paul saying that all his past achievements were 'garbage' (Phil. 3:8) but the Greek word could be translated as something stronger than that! Again, where is the line? In any joke there is an exchange between listener and speaker. Is it the speaker's responsibility not to offend, or the listener's not to be offended? I don't have an easy answer, other than to say that I didn't want to be in the same room as some of the 'jokes' and anecdotes I heard. I felt polluted by them. This is despite being a man of the world with forty years of totally secular living under his belt.

Some of the jokes were so offensive that it made me yearn for one of those lame vicar-jokes we hear on a Sunday. But the incidents also made me wonder if, as a Christian, I had lost my sense of humour. It's a tough one. Perhaps I have. Or is it that I just don't find some things funny any more? I didn't have a great sense that God was outraged. It was that I felt what was happening in front of me was horrible.

So, where does the line come? We live in an age where outrage can be sparked and careers ended.

STAND-UP AND BE COUNTED

I don't want to be someone who is on a knife-edge of offence, and I do not want to be offensive. It is a complicated time and issue. But the question is, are some things beyond the reach of humour?

It wasn't just the jokes, of course. We all have a world view. But I found myself feeling sad as I unpicked some of the world views on offer. They are the usual panel of failed ways of doing life. Hedonism was a big one: 'Let's hear a cheer for me. I can now drink three bottles of rosé in one sitting.' Then there was stoicism. The routine here would form around how rubbish life is and that we had better just put up with it and get to the end as quickly as possible.

But despite the dark side, so many of the comedians I saw were asking genuine questions about how to live life and what makes for a good one. I loved their questions and their bravery in tackling some tough subjects. Comedy can and does get close to the edge, and the comedy I saw reminded me that in my preaching I might be bolder and help people to see the funny side of some of the difficulties we all go through.

In a desire to be nice and liked, the danger is that we iron out offence. Perhaps the key is to generate good offence and not the kind that diminishes individuals. We need to earn the right to be offensive, perhaps, and any offence needs to be based in truth.

Study questions

It is easy to do church in a bubble. It is equally easy to demonize the world of comedy . . .

What do you think we can learn from the world of comedy? How might church benefit from some of the tools and techniques of the comedian?

Comedy tends to take risks with anecdotes. It often stretches an anecdote beyond where we might think it would go.

Do you think we are sometimes too nice and inoffensive? How might we use anecdote in speaking to others?

I didn't want to be in the same room as some of the 'jokes' and anecdotes I heard . . . This is despite being a man of the world with forty years of totally secular living under his belt.

Do you find yourself unable to join in with some of the world's 'jokes'? Do you ever feel compromised about this?

Prayer

Thank you for the creativity and vitality of comedy. Thank you that we have others who want to make us laugh and to see the world in different ways. Can you help us to learn from comedy, and not to see it as somehow separate from the life of faith? Let us reach out in friendship and appreciation to those who work in the arts, and help our churches to be places of risk where we are prepared to encourage laughter.

13

Bring on the Clowns

Back in the 1990s, a curious movement began in the church. There was an outbreak of clowns. It is interesting to wonder why such a thing occurred and why it happened just then. Perhaps the church was beginning to take itself too seriously, and it was a case of 'clowns to the rescue'. But it might equally be that clowns found a worthy spokesperson who could articulate why the church so needed them and what God might think about it

> Back in the 1990s, a curious movement began in the church. There was an outbreak of clowns.

all. That spokesperson issued a rallying cry for a dose of foolishness and for seeing afresh the 'foolishness of God' (1 Cor. 1:25). After all, the creator of the universe took the risky decision to be born as one of us – not the kind of temperate, sensible decision one might expect from the Great CEO.

Roly Bain was both a priest and a clown. Indeed, for a while, he was actually a regular parish priest, but he had been bitten by the clowning bug, and he had begun to wonder if the church needed shaking up. He resigned his parish in 1990 and spent a year at clown school. For the rest of his career he was an itinerant, travelling from church to church, performance to performance.

What's particularly interesting about Bain's ministry and success is that it was accompanied by a fully thought-through theology that explained the power of foolishness and saw deep connections between the character and experience of clowns and the character and experience of Jesus himself. Bain saw that clowning was both a metaphor for the journey of faith and a safety valve for church, and that if we might embrace it, then we might see a different kind of church evolving.

Bain was certainly a tonic. He claimed to have flung custard pies into the faces of ten serving bishops and that most of them, he said, were grateful (although that may have been wishful thinking). He would process into church dressed as his clown alter-ego Holy Roly in a multicoloured costume, waving a feather duster, riding a unicycle and wearing an outsized dog collar. As he reached the lectern, he would invite the congregation into his presence with: 'Let us play!'

If it had just been a case of flinging together a few circus tricks and a red nose, it would surely have been not much more than an irritating gimmick. But behind the costume was a profound set of insights.

There are two key kinds of clown. There is the *auguste* – the simpleton, who has emotions close to the surface and is frequently knocked back and over. The auguste is clumsy, messy and the butt of the jokes. They have the knack of being in the wrong place at the wrong time. They are the idiot and the fool.

And then there is the *whiteface*, with his white canonical hat and set of musical instruments. The whiteface is arrogant, pompous, powerful and humourless. The whiteface stands for figures of authority and seriousness and being all grown-up.

In the clown world, the dynamic between the whiteface and the auguste underscores a more general battle, and one which the Christian faith deeply

BRING ON THE CLOWNS 155

understands. The struggle between the auguste and the whiteface symbolizes the eternal battle between the powers of oppression and control and the counterbalance of freedom to make mistakes, be foolish and childlike. When you think about it, this is a familiar dynamic in the Gospels – the authorities v. the unlikely fool.

In this battlefield, the clown is the great debunker and nonconformist. The auguste punctures the pompous and bounces back from seemingly impossible odds, always with love for others. And in this, the clown harks back to the age of jesters and courts and kings. Bain saw his clowning as part of a great and ancient tradition in the church and in the world, where even the king's court had used the services of a jester. The ancient church allowed the Feast of Fools – a brief period each year when the church turned itself on its head, dressed up and generally mocked and challenged authority. For Bain, if it was good enough for them, then there was no reason not to create a bit of havoc in the modern church.

In this clash between the auguste and the whiteface, Bain saw the dynamic of Jesus and his ministry. The auguste is like Jesus. The whiteface represents the religious authorities Jesus took on. The clown somehow keeps that dynamic going and, while Jesus got himself killed, for Bain it was a chance to allow the church to breathe again and experience the wonder of God who was on the side of the lost, the lonely and the foolish.

The clown can talk to power and show that the world needs to be upside down. The clown is the truth-teller (rather as today's truth-tellers tend to be stand-up comedians). They show us that even grown-ups can play.

The life of a clown

Bain died very young at just 62 years of age. His life and career were quite remarkable, especially for the dent he made on the way church saw itself, at least for a while. Bain co-founded Holy Fools,[1] a network of clowns, and his ministry was sponsored by the then Archbishop of Canterbury, George Carey. Holy Roly 'appeared' at the Lambeth Conference in 1998. Goodness only knows what they made of him. Can you imagine a clown being invited these days? It seems that we are, perhaps, too serious and preoccupied with the issues the church faces to take a moment out to watch someone with flappy shoes and a giant red nose.

Bain wrote some very thoughtful books, and he helped the church to wonder if we needed to hear more laughter during the service and to be able to take ourselves more lightly.

Indeed, he once said of the first church he attended, St Mary's Barnes: 'I learned that you could laugh in church', and that church ritual 'had to be done in a sort of tongue-in-cheek way.'[2]

The flip side of comedy is, of course, tragedy, and the clown knows this well. Bain was really saying that the church has to give people permission to laugh and cry – just as clowns do. If church allows that honesty and release, then we might be able to go deeper with God rather than remain at a polite distance from him and each other.

You cannot have comedy without tragedy, and tragedy's close sibling is comedy. For Bain, this is what made the presence of clowns in church so profound – they held in tension the two poles of our experience, and the eternal tussle in the Christian story between the tragedy of the cross and the joy and foolishness of the resurrection.

Clown-friendly church

What might church be like if the clowns had more of a say? Bain's would set up a slack-wire between two poles topped with crosses. His battle to stay on the wire acted a telling metaphor for the wobbliness of all of our faiths. It was a communication technique, but the sheer peril of it also brought home the peril of a God who risked everything, and the peril of taking a step of faith. If we embrace the wobbliness of the faith journey, then it becomes a bit less scary and more on a human scale. Humour has a way of getting things into perspective and helping us to remember the stories we hear in church.

Bain would carry out intercessions by blowing bubbles consisting of washing-up liquid. As they popped, he would encourage the congregation to understand that God had popped the bubbles because he had heard the prayers.

The clown holds up a possibility for a church that is less tight than it tends to be. A clown wouldn't suit every church, of course. Indeed, a weekly dose of clowning might become a bit tiresome. Some of us are a bit more serious and a clown with silly shoes and a trumpet might not exactly help us to get closer to God.

But I want to say that a church without clowns might be a poorer place. Or perhaps the church without a clowning instinct might risk being dry and lifeless.

The church that at least takes on some of the world view of the clown might be an interesting prospect.

To have the ability to be creative, less organized, to see things from upside down, and to have the ability to laugh at ourselves and the great 'foolishness of God' (1 Cor. 1:25) might be a very good thing. Clowns always dust themselves down and start again – and any church needs a bit of this resurrection spirit about it.

The clown represents the triumph of hope over experience and the defeat of paternalism and orderliness. A church that was all-clown, all chaotic auguste would, of course, be a disaster. Nothing would get done. Mistake would be piled upon mistake, and you can only fall over so many times before it begins to hurt. We might lose some of the times of silence and reflection and we might alienate people. But is there an opportunity for a little clown DNA to be added to our church make-up?

That Jesus had much in common with beautiful chaos and the love of the clown is a very compelling idea. The close identification between Roly Bain and his Lord helps us to see the joy and tragedy of the gospel story. And the ancient figure of the court jester, able to speak to power, might prevent any church from lurching into disasters brought about by an inward focus of elevated notions of self.

The last church clowns

There is something sad that I have to report. Buoyed-up by a level of excitement about the possibility of being more aligned with clowns, I decided to contact the organization that Bain co-founded. Neil Wilkin, current chair of Holy Fools, told me that the climate had shifted – this being 2019, pre-Covid. A fear of the phenomenon of scary clowns had had an impact on the number of Christians wanting to be clowns, and the lack of youngsters in church made the potential for appearing there less enticing.

Wilkin told me that there were only two ordained people who were still performing clowns, and one of these was past retirement age.

We have a shortage of clowns in the church. Are we approaching the time where there is not a single ordained clown? That would be sad indeed.

Study questions

Bain saw that clowning was both a metaphor for the journey of faith and a safety valve for church, and that if we might embrace it, then we might see a different kind of church evolving.

What do you think of this? What might the connection be between church and clowning?

Indeed, he once said of the first church he attended, St Mary's Barnes: 'I learned that you could laugh in church', and that church ritual 'had to be done in a sort of tongue-in-cheek way.'

What might church be like if we let the influence of clown come into play?

The close identification between Roly Bain and his Lord helps us to see the joy and tragedy of the gospel story.

What connections are there between the Gospels and the clown?

Prayer

Dear Father, we are grateful for clowns and see the great connection between the way clowns look at the world and the way our Lord did too. May we have an attitude that helps us to puncture seriousness and pomposity.

14

Foolish Saint: Martin Luther

When we think about the greats of Christian comedy, I don't believe that Martin Luther, father of the Reformation, is the first person to spring to mind. Indeed, the humour of Luther is almost totally ignored by scholars. But anyone involved in the Diet of Worms must have something going for them.

In fact, Luther and his humour cover so many bases that to ignore him and his mirth would be to miss one of the greats. Indeed, he joins a long line of 'saints' with a funny bone. In the third century, St Lawrence, who was burned to death on a grill over hot coals, is reputed to have called out to his executioners, 'Turn me over . . . I'm done on this side!'[1]

Of course, he had a much, much darker side and antisemitism is just one of the areas, which we must never forget. But here, let's look at his mirth, which operates on many levels. Perhaps the most interesting is the way a change in how he saw himself in relation to God opened up a new way of life and spirituality – and that way was marked by deep mirth. This was despite the fact that he lived in perilous times. Plague was a constant threat, not to mention the attentions of the authorities. Luther was able to get to a place where – despite having a depressive and anxious nature and being surrounded by difficulties – he could rely on his mirth to give him perspective and carry out his ministry.

As a young man, Luther was full of anxiety. His faith gave him no joy. In fact, quite the opposite. He drove himself half-mad as he became obsessed with his own sinfulness. He punished himself and obsessively did penances, but to no avail. In the end he came to almost hate God. He could find no relief at all. He was as far away from a light-hearted mirth as it was possible to be.

But he had a spiritual breakthrough that changed his life and his demeanor. Having taken wise counsel

FOOLISH SAINT: MARTIN LUTHER

and gone back to his Bible, he realized that it was through faith alone that he was saved and could be free. He described this as being 'born again'.[2] God was on his side and not his enemy and he could live life again.

A kind of odd joy and serenity overtook him. Despite all his turbulent times, he retained an abiding sense of humour. If, through Christ, he was at peace with God, he could be at peace with himself. Allied to this was the sense he had that life is short and eternity waits. He was liberated from a long-term depression to a newness of life focused on justification by faith alone.

If life is short, then we can be light with the things we are faced with. We can see their absurdity and be freed from too much seriousness.

There is something rather profound here – that a church's and a people's humour springs not from an abstract sense of fun and the odd joke; instead, we can relax into mirth and merriment because we have a sense of security in God and how he feels towards us.

The newly mirthful Luther began to use his humour everywhere. He saw himself as something of a court jester. He used humour to ridicule his many enemies. He was outraged at the many ecclesiastical abuses he saw. He decided that the best form of attack was humour. He dressed in an odd costume when meeting a papal representative in order to mislead him into thinking that the pope had nothing to fear. He took on his arch-rival, Archbishop Albrecht of Mainz, and his love of relics. (Mainz was looking to raise more money from the poor to buy even more of them.) Luther wrote a satirical pamphlet outlining some of the new relics that would be purchased. These included a lock of the 'devil's beard' and flames from the burning bush.[3]

When offering pastoral care, Luther was also known to make light of his charges' afflictions and help them to get some perspective on things.

Uncomfortable humour

Luther used a kind of humour many modern Christians would be uncomfortable with. We like our humour clean and we also quite like polite, if sometimes biting, wit. It has perhaps always been so. Luther was obsessed with the toilet and with what went on there. His humour was, to say the least, earthy.

> Luther used a kind of humour many modern Christians would be uncomfortable with.

There is a reason why Luther used such language. In his time it was more normal to have a realized sense of the actual presence of the devil. He was prowling around (1 Pet. 5:8). The devil 'understood' filth. He traded in it. So a right response to him getting close was to use the kind of language and images that he understood.

If we want to reach out with mirth and merriment beyond a polite, metropolitan audience, do we need to be a bit more 'liberal' with the kind of humour we welcome into the envelope of the holy? What would we make of the anecdote that Luther shared with his beloved wife just before he died? Personally, it made my day and made me laugh out loud.

> I'm like a ripe stool and the world's like a gigantic anus, and we're about to let go of each other.[4]

Study questions

. . . how he saw himself in relation to God opened up a new way of life and spirituality – and that way was marked by deep mirth.

How does conversion lead to mirth? Can being a person of faith help you to be a person of mirth?

A kind of odd joy and serenity overtook him. Despite all his turbulent times, he retained an abiding sense of humour. If, through Christ, he was at peace with God, he could be at peace with himself.

Have you ever experienced serenity and humour in difficult times.

When offering pastoral care, Luther was also known to make light of his charges' afflictions and help them to get some perspective on things.

How can humour and mirth help us in dealing with other people who need our help?

Prayer

Father, we don't usually associate this great person of the faith, Luther, with humour and mirth. We thank you for his attitude of merriment and his understanding of the need to see the funny side of things. Help us to learn from his example.

---

# 15

The Holy Fool: St Francis

> The size of a man's understanding may always be justly measured by his mirth.
>
> *Samuel Johnson*[1]

An idea has haunted these pages – the 'foolishness of God' (1 Cor. 1:25). Of course, the very idea sounds outrageous, and perhaps even insulting to the deity. How could the mighty God present himself and his ways as foolish? But the evidence stalks the passages of the Bible.

THE HOLY FOOL: ST FRANCIS

In Hebrew Scripture, the prophets make a point through their foolishness. The naked Jeremiah flounces through Jerusalem. He spends time in a muddy water cistern (Jer. 38:6). In the New Testament, John the Baptist looks a frightful mess and eats honey and locusts (Matt. 3:4).

Christ's message is foolish to those who are sophisticated and know the way the world really is. His radical declarations of nonviolence, loving your enemies (Matt. 5:44) and the like sounded hopelessly naïve – they still do.

St Paul acknowledges how silly the Christian way really seems (1 Cor. 1:18–25). He says that, to the wise, it looks foolish. And indeed, it did and does. For a clever man like him, this must have been either a deep agony, or a glorious sense of the ridiculous. Paul could have been humiliated in Athens by the sophistication of the philosophical arguments and people he met with. His message didn't really work there. But he carried on, in the knowledge that sophistication and eloquence is no defence against the foolish ways and love of God.

Paul calls the followers to be 'fools for Christ' (1 Cor. 4:10) and for a serious man like Paul, that was probably a blessed release. But can we listen to that call today? What would it look like for us to be truly foolish?

What's more, Paul acknowledges that early followers were not a shiny, successful lot. The faith attracted people who weren't powerful. They were mainly ordinary urban dwellers – but God uses their sheer ordinariness to 'shame the strong' (1 Cor. 1:26–29). It was always thus.

God did something that looked foolish, and he still does – he works through the marginalized, the odd, the broken and the weak. And his chief fool was he himself – Christ, the 'fool' who changed the world. There was another fool, who became a saint, who also worked for the Lord.

St Francis

St Francis, as we know him now, was born into a *nouveau riche* family (c. 1181). His father was a wealthy and successful cloth merchant. Francis's early life was relatively standard fare. He got himself into trouble, served in the army and generally had a high time. But a revelation of God led to a sharp change of direction. But even before that he had been influenced by things that in turn influenced his later ministry.

THE HOLY FOOL: ST FRANCIS

As a boy, troubadours and *jongleurs* seized his imagination. The troubadours composed love songs and poems singing of courtly love and knights and ladies. They were wandering entertainers – romantic, exciting and strange. *Jongleurs* didn't compose, but did sing the songs and poems of others. Young Francis was transfixed.

Francis's change of direction led to him setting up an Order of travelling friars, who became known as the Fools for Christ. Much of his work consisted of rebuilding churches. But what sets him apart is the behaviour of both him and his followers. This was marked by unpredictability, exuberance and the true mark of the fool: doing the thing you'd least expect and seemed to be the most stupid.

Francis wasn't one for book learning. He never became a priest and never owned a complete Bible, but his foolish mission changed the church and still has an influence today. Francis drew his inspiration from St Paul's simple call in 1 Corinthians 4:10: 'We are fools for Christ . . .'

Francis's foolishness extended to stripping off his clothes in public, appearing naked in church, renouncing wealth and befriending a range of creatures. It also involved him taming a much-feared wolf and walking unarmed across Egypt to the sultan's camp during the Crusades. What is our equivalent of walking unarmed into the den of a powerful enemy and offering love and reconciliation?

Why on earth would he do such things? From what impulse? It certainly wasn't a desire to show off or be outrageous for the sake of it. Instead, it came from a deep connection with Christ. He realized that the fool had to accept humiliations, just as Christ had. These helped the world to see things upside down. His foolishness was a deep comment on the rich and the powerful, and to show that we need not cling to all of the regular securities when we have God.

Francis was not afraid to laugh and cry and exchange his clothes with a filthy beggar; he could not help but do such things because of the joy and exuberance and overflowing of emotion brought on by an acceptance of God's beautiful grace and a joy in God's love.

Francis's action sprang from spiritual truth and emotionalism, and this is perhaps uncomfortable. His jollity and foolishness were contagious – these things generally are. When one person laughs, it is hard not to join in.

If we are to build a church fit for fools and ready for mirth and jollity, would it be more emotional than

THE HOLY FOOL: ST FRANCIS

the church we have at present? Where would we catch that spontaneity, even in a liturgical context? Mirth and jollity cannot be manufactured and still ring true. Francis taught us that the spontaneity of mirth and sadness come from the same place – and the church has made up its mind not to forget his beautiful contribution and humble soul.

> Mirth and jollity cannot be manufactured and still ring true.

Study questions

Francis drew his inspiration from St Paul's simple call in 1 Corinthians 4:10: 'We are fools for Christ . . .'

What might it mean to be 'fools for Christ'?

Francis was not afraid to laugh and cry and exchange his clothes with a filthy beggar; he could not help but do such things because of the joy and exuberance and overflowing of emotion brought on by an acceptance of God's beautiful grace and a joy in God's love.

How can joy and exuberance be part of our faith life?

Mirth and jollity cannot be manufactured and still ring true. Francis taught us that the spontaneity of mirth and sadness come from the same place – and the church has made up its mind not to forget his beautiful contribution and humble soul.

Where have you encountered spontaneity in life, work and church?

Prayer

Thank you for the great saint. Can we learn from Francis's love, spontaneity and openness? Help us to be vulnerable like him and open to the Spirit of God. May our foolishness inspire others.

PART FOUR

The Renewed Church

16

Building the Merry and Mirthful Church

That great old biblical king David was not immune to controversy. At one point he brings the ire of his own family upon himself. Overcome with gratefulness to God, he dances in public. It is a kind of worship. His wife is mortified. She despises him. His behaviour is like that of a 'vulgar fellow', and not the king (1 Sam. 6:12–20). She has fallen victim to a common prejudice – that solemnity is more godly than merriment.

In some way this whole quest has been asking what the merry and mirthful church looks like. That is the church I think I would go to if I were wondering what to do on a Sunday.

Of course, fake mirth and merriment is deeply unpleasant. It is to be discouraged. Church's prime purpose is not entertainment – although it can be entertaining. And mirth and merriment are more than possible in even the highest of churches. Indeed, I have sometimes found myself deeply miserable amidst the hurly-burly and smiles of charismatic worship.

Author and priest Fergus Butler-Gallie emailed me with some help on what the church I have been reaching for might look like.

> What of the Church – well I suppose it looks basically like this: taking God seriously means it is no longer possible for us to take ourselves seriously. I'm not particularly a fan of 'fun liturgy' as I think it flips that the other way round. What I think is needed is an authentic joy in the foibles and follies of the life God has given us. I think an acknowledgement of our own ridiculousness helps to make us more attractive, keeps the commands of Christ and, crucially, magnifies the effects of grace. So, from bishops I think that means less managerialism, more witty asides; from clergy, less angst, more joy, and from God's people,

> I think it means more of an understanding of Christian life being an infectious one of joy rather than something we do for an hour on Sunday.[1]

The more I read this, the more I think that Fergus is right. Life is full of foibles, and so are we and the people we share the planet with. When we lose our sense of humour about such things, we begin to get bitter and dried-up. But as King David found, appearing absurd carries risks (not the least of which is annoying our loved ones).

Is it possible to find ourselves ridiculous? I frequently find myself so. One option is to despair that I am not more shiny, polished, or proficient. But, actually, I very frequently mess things up. I say the wrong thing. I cannot think my way out of a paper bag.

But what if that ridiculousness is actually what makes me special? Is it *that* which God finds most lovable? I think it might be. God might prefer the golfer who takes 116 on the first hole, lands in water and breaks their club to the one who gets the hole in one. What golfer needs to pray when every ball is hit right down the middle?

Plus, of course, the things that make us ridiculous do require a lot of grace; grace towards ourselves, and grace from others towards us. I made the biggest breakthrough of my own life when I realized that my father was not annoying, he was funny.

From that day on I was like a child with him again. I revelled in his foibles and loved them, and him. My anger melted. I said goodbye to judgementalism and just enjoyed him as he was. It was a case of taking the big old plank out of my eye (Matt. 7:3–5). I very much regret taking so long to make this breakthrough – just six months before he died of motor neurone disease. But those six months were some of the best of our lives as we began laughing together and finding each other funny again.

Fergus calls out bishops to be more playful and less managerial. It is a thing I have heard often; I do feel a bit sorry for bishops who have a huge managerial task and would be remiss to ignore or downplay it. But more fun is good for everyone and might make a bishop feel less lonely and less pressured to be all things to all people.

Then, Fergus asks priests to ditch some of the angst and earnestness and discover some joy and playfulness. These are good thoughts. The stern priest, the priest who seems to be full of judgement, is no advert for the faith. It takes courage to be playful, though. An experienced priest once advised me not to let the congregation see who I truly was; I should show no weakness, or they would tear me apart. It sounded odd to me at the time and I haven't taken that advice! But I understand the impulse – protect yourself. Yet, we are called not to do so, and that means being able to be light and joyful and plain silly. And that, of course, is much more than telling a joke at the start of the service.

Plus, Fergus asks congregations to be less focused on Sunday and more aware of the Christian life each day – one of joy and mirth. Why not? What have we to lose? Amid the dire, and I think much overblown, warnings about the fate of the church, an outbreak of merriment is surely worth cultivating.

Another conversation, this time with James Cary, author of *The Sacred Art of Joking*, confirms what I've been thinking. He advises me that the track we need is marked with a glorious absurdity.

> Life is absurd, God's Word is often funny . . . God made it that way on purpose. Being caught up in the absurdity of life is part of our humanity.

> Of course, churches don't always make it easy for us to revel in absurdity – except unintentionally.

> The architecture and art of church tends towards the sombre. We feel like naughty schoolchildren

if we laugh. The dry reading style people adopt for public Bible reading makes it dead and then there are the sermons which are just a list of dos and don'ts. But Jesus calls us to merriment. It's a command. When he was around all the holy people kept telling him off for it.[2]

So perhaps that is our starting point – a rediscovery of the absurdity of life and ourselves – tempered, of course, by the knowledge of just how precious we are to God. The march towards the merry and mirthful church might just begin with the banana skin.

> Perhaps that is our starting point – a rediscovery of the absurdity of life.

When I used to play cricket, it was a sheer joy to be with the team. We laughed so much that we ached. We enjoyed each other's foibles and we were able to be ourselves. It was a place of camaraderie and developed into a fellowship of care for each other. We loved the thrill of winning, but didn't mind if we lost. We enjoyed heading to the pub afterwards for a pint and some reflection on the heroism of our performances. It was an environment that had depth and flavour, and as I slogged through work each week, I couldn't wait for a game of cricket at the weekend. It became an alternative family.

There is a lot to be said for the pub as a good model for jollity, foolishness and mirth. The medieval writers would sometimes draw a series of inferences from the parable of the good Samaritan (Luke 10:25–37). The good Samaritan is Jesus. The wounded man is all humankind – knocked over by sin – and the place of refuge (the church) is the inn. It is a place where the bar tab has been paid; a place of safety.

There is a perception among some that Christians have a tendency to be killjoys – lacking a sense of humour. If this is true, then we might be waiting a long time for mirth, foolishness and jollity to break out in church. But author Elton Trueblood argues otherwise: 'Any alleged Christianity which fails to express itself in gaiety, at some point, is clearly spurious.'[3]

In other words, we might expect jollity at any point of contact with the church because our faith is geared towards joy, even in the face of what the world has to throw at us. Joy is at the heart of the faith, and that means that this joy, this jollity is, or should be, part of our experience of being part of a church community. We don't ignore our own suffering, or the sufferings of the world, but we can look at them through the lens of eternity, and that lens helps us to feel a little mirth even in the darkest hour.

BUILDING THE MERRY CHURCH

The hope of heaven is a strong theological and doctrinal anchor for the presence of merriment and mirth in a church. Perhaps, if they are missing, we have lost sight of the fact that we are on the way home.

So, where might we look for the next outbreak of mirth and foolishness? Are we due one? It certainly looks like it. Outbreaks of mirth and foolishness tend to be a reaction to a church that begins to be insular and takes itself too seriously.

Is it fair to say that the church has become stuck on certain subjects? If it has become so, then a little light relief may actually be a more profound comment than we imagine. What do our disagreements – often carried out in shrill and remorseless voices – about human sexuality and the like say to those who watch us from afar?

There has been an outbreak of books urging the church to loosen up, search for saints in unlikely places and generally let its hair down. These tend to be books that urge us to start again and to think again. I am cautious about these. As an ex-brand consultant, I remember that the easiest opinions to hold and express are those of the 'Well, I wouldn't start from here!' variety. The problem is that we *are* starting from here, and simply ushering in blue-sky thinking is unlikely to get us very far. It is easy to be a rebel and renegade when your ideas will never happen and you know it.

The Charismatic Movement and humour

Having come to faith in a Pentecostal church, you might imagine that I would say that such an expression of spirituality is an ideal way of engendering some humour. People waving flags, speaking in tongues[4] and dancing in the Spirit is a ready-made comedy opportunity. I still love my friends from that wing of the church, and admire them tremendously. But I am not sure that they would see what they are doing as funny or mirthful. But then again, the kind of unpredictable outpourings in the modern Pentecostal Church go right back to the unpredictable ministry of St Francis of Assisi.

The Franciscan's escapades were not about show, but were a kind of childlike emotionalism that was much-needed for a church that had become over-intellectual and over-ritualized. They were much frowned upon by the Benedictines. The Rule of St Benedict doesn't encourage anything that leads to much laughter, but doesn't wholly forbid merriment.[5]

The modern charismatic movement has ancient roots and is to be welcomed. But its main focus is not mirth, and that is fine but isn't quite what we are looking for in this book.

The Messy Movement – mirth as iconoclasm

Mike Yaconelli's *Messy Spirituality: Christianity for the Rest of Us*[6] was an instant classic. Its winning picture of how the spiritual journey is intrinsically messy and chaotic encouraged individuals and churches to be more tolerant of mistakes, and to embrace humour even if much of that was unintentional.

Yaconelli points out that Jesus did battle with those who saw themselves as perfect spiritual people and urges us all to let go of seeking perfection. This anti-perfection is, maybe, the gateway to some degree of mirth and jolliness. Yaconelli describes his congregation as a bit of a rabble, a truly mixed bunch. People who are messy and whose lives are nowhere near perfect, but who all wanted a spiritual life that was real.

The church that results with Mike Yaconelli is a riot of unpredictability. But it wouldn't, of course, suit everyone. It is OK to be sorted and well-organized and respectable and love God and go to a sorted, respected and well-organized church.

Other writers have mined this seam of unconventional church for messy people. Nadia Bolz-Weber's *Accidental Saints: Finding God in all the Wrong People*[7] is cut from the same kind of cloth as *Messy Spirituality*. It is an engaging look at messy people and their connection with God. Dave Tomlinson's *How to Be a Bad Christian*[8] again prompts us to turn church upside down. But he does so with a keen eye to the rebirth of mirth. He wonders if God might actually be fond of beer and rude jokes.

Luther, of course, would have signed up to the rude jokes and beer manifesto like a shot. Indeed, he may have been made life honorary president.

For me, at least, while these are intriguing ways of confronting sterility in the church, they are too narrow to truly see a more extensive outbreak of jollity, mirth and foolishness. What we need is not a clown in every pulpit, or a self-confessed messy minister, but an attitude that allows the light of mirth into any situation, with gentleness. It is perfectly possible to be a church that doesn't take itself too seriously in a liturgical setting. It is equally possible to look for excellence and also be open to foolishness and mirth. Or at least, I hope it is.

Perhaps a new outbreak of mirth, foolishness and jollity is a possibility in the church just as it is. We don't need to knock the walls down – we just need to open ourselves up a little more, accepting that there is time for seriousness and silence and all the other things we love about church.

Foolishness and mirth in the established church

The funniest, most mirthful experience I ever had of church was on my placement at one of the great cathedrals while I was training to be a vicar. My mentor (who has gone on to be my friend) was a bishop. He had a huge sense of the importance of the Sacrament and the need to take preaching seriously and to work at it. And yet I laughed more on that placement than I have ever done elsewhere.

He and his colleagues had a keen sense of the ridiculous and the ability to mouth a quiet levity in moments of seriousness. They understood that mistakes weren't the end of the world. They knew that people trying to be on their best behaviour in a very serious building sometimes said unfortunate and funny things. And they knew that people on edge before worship can be put at their ease by a kindly word and a gentle piece of humour. The baby does not need to be thrown out with the bathwater.

It isn't that we have to start again to create a new mirth movement, or encourage more foolishness.

We start with what we have and learn from the architects of humour. Part of humour is humility – the opposite of pomposity and pride. God's kingdom is an upside-down affair, and so we can perhaps begin our search for the Church of Mirth by encouraging an outbreak of humility.

One way of bringing more mirth and foolishness into church is not to manufacture it – we have already noted that to attempt to do so rings a note of falsehood. Having a stand-up comedian leading the service each week would get very wearing (as are the vicar jokes). The art is to spot the humour that is simple happenstance – church will manufacture humour quite naturally.

My wish is that vicars might not need to start their sermons with a joke, and might instead embody a lightness, humour and a mirthful disposition.

But there's something else. Can we live with eccentricity? Has our church become uniform? Has anyone else noted the standard evangelical worship leaders' uniforms of the checked shirt and sensible shoes? When people are truly free of fear and free in Christ, then they can be their eccentric self, and perhaps that is the real measure of how we are doing. If there was an eccentricity swingometer, how would your church score? Can we be ourselves in church?

If we are feeling depressed, can we admit it? Are we able to ditch the false smiles and be truly ourselves? Because if we could, even in our bad moments we'd be pretty funny.

If we are set free in Christ, we are set free to not care less what people think of us. Bishop Michael Colclough said these wise words:[9]

> When you have confidence in God – deep confidence in him – then it is liberating and you don't need to be frightened of others and their reactions. You can be yourself. Think about when God says of Jesus when he is baptized, 'This is my beloved, with him I am well pleased.' [see Matt. 17:5] You cannot say it literally without a smile on your face. That reminds us of the divine smile when God looks at us. God is delighted in us. That means that even if we are going through a hard time, then there is a bedrock of happiness in our lives. And that means a propensity to jollity.

Merriment can signal a fresh start

The great football manager and player Brian Clough had a blip in his career. The forty-four days he served as Leeds United's coach in 1974 were marked by bad feeling. He got the sack. It looked like it was the end of Clough – although he lived to fight another day. He was followed at Leeds by that wise old manager, Jimmy Armfield, who found himself faced with turmoil. The atmosphere in the club seemed toxic. What was he to do? He had a plan.

With the help of a theatre producer, he put on a pantomime starring himself and the players and sold tickets to the fans.[10] Many of the players were dressed in drag. Hard-man Billy Bremner was cast as Buttons. Playing against type, Norman Hunter was Prince Charming. Perhaps Armfield hoped that a dose of foolishness might help people to feel more normal with each other. It is barely believable that something as simple as an outbreak of merriment could be seen as the cure for a club that had forgotten who and what it was. Surely, it wouldn't happen now! These days we might call in an army of management consultants. But so it was back then.

The pantomime did the trick. That season the club reached the final of the European Cup.

I sometimes wonder if at church we might take a leaf out of the Armfield book of fresh starts. Why don't we take a moment away from seriousness and discipleship and whatever and simply enjoy something mirthful and merry? A dance, a game, bingo (without the gambling) or a knees-up can all help us

BUILDING THE MERRY CHURCH

to reconnect with one another and realize that we actually like each other. Uncomplicated merriment at church is godly because we have a God who is merry and encourages it in others.

If the Trinity is a kind of divine party, then we might feel free to join in.

Study questions

Fergus asks congregations to be less focused on Sunday and more aware of the Christian life each day – one of joy and mirth. Why not? What have we to lose?

Well – what *have* we to lose? Can we concentrate more on the whole week rather than just Sunday?

Is it fair to say that the church has become stuck on certain subjects? If it has become so, then a little light relief may actually be a more profound comment than we imagine.

What kind of comment might that be? How might mirth change the church?

Perhaps a new outbreak of mirth, foolishness and jollity is a possibility in the church just as it is. We don't need to knock the walls down – we just need to open ourselves up a little more, accepting that there is time for seriousness and silence and all the other things we love about church.

What might opening ourselves up to mirth look like? How might the church respond and change in this way over the coming years?

Prayer

Lord, will you lead us and help us to open up our church to more mirth and merriment? We are excited by what this might look like and want you to show us. Help us to see good examples from elsewhere and be open to change but also be open to keeping all that is good that we already have. Let people who have never come to church know that they will find something life-affirming and fun when they come through our doors.

17

Signing Up to the Mirth Manifesto

So, what might a mirth manifesto look like? Would it get your vote?

Take the temperature – where are you starting from?

Where are you and your church on the spectrum of mirth and merriment? Being jolly, accepting, kind and quirky are markers of the mirthful and merry life and church. Those words have a lot of currency. It seems to me that they can work in any church context – from the most to the least liturgical. This is because they are about attitudes to life and church and to people – and of course, to God.

Sign up to 'faith, hope and love'

Mirth and merriment separated out from a world view are just fleeting experiences – moments that have come and gone. Perhaps this is why mirth and merriment can get a bit of a bad press. It is the serious folk that seem to get recognized as profound.

But if these things spring from a view of the world that has 'faith, hope and love' at the centre (1 Cor. 13:13), then they will be infused with the kind of joy that is shared with others and is irresistible to all. In short, the Christian world view seems uniquely placed to proclaim and live out merriment and mirth and to make it a communal activity. It does that because it is not primarily about doctrine or even ideas. It is instead about the *person* of God and the story of his wooing of personkind.

And at the heart of it all is a deep and abiding grace. It would be hard not to have some mirth and merriment in church if we also knew that God is full of grace. Of course, if a church has lost sight of that grace, then it too might be judgemental, tight and lacking in mirth.

Church is, of course, communal. When done well, it is the kind of family into which all are welcomed and accepted. If church is like this, then we notice merriment being shared around. So, the church is an antidote to privatization. The privatization of faith, the life lived in a bubble of holiness is, to me at least, a sad thing.

See mirth in creation and the incarnation

It seems that mirth and merriment may be hardwired into the very fabric and building blocks of the world. The idea that creation is having a ginormous party – all the time – is both charming and deeply profound. It might account for the way we get that odd feeling of wonderment in the presence of nature. When we watch our pets being themselves, or the birds in the garden or see a magnificent tree, it is easy to think that their very lives are a kind of song of praise to the creator God.

Similarly, if the incarnation means anything, then it means that Jesus was not *pretending* to be a human being. If he was one of us, truly one of us, and the best version of one of us, it is impossible that he did not live out a life of mirth and merriment. He did so, even though he sometimes felt sad and angry and fearful – just like us.

Perhaps we need to reimagine the Trinity. We might do well to picture the laughing Messiah, imagine the Holy Spirit whispering a word into our ears to celebrate and be merry, and see God the Father as the loving parent who smiles at his children.

Perhaps we can sign up to the knowledge that mirth and merriment are both a picture of the coming kingdom of God and a marker of the Christian life well-lived.

Be prepared to be surprised – and take risks

Mirth has a certain abandon about it – merriment is also something that tends to take us beyond the familiar. If, as a church, we want to be more mirthful, we may need to be prepared to be surprised where it might take us. The experiments in some UK cathedrals were not without risk and garnered criticism. But I admire the initiatives because they came from people who were prepared to try something and take a risk.

Perhaps, in the aftermath of the coronavirus pandemic, it will be time to open up 'church' at the local pub or coffee shop, or to open the doors to theatre or the performing arts.

In many ways it depends where you are starting from and who you are starting with. It may be that your church has lost the knack of being mirthful, which can be very sad. But if the sound of simple laughter and enjoyment of each other's company has become a distant memory, then it might be time to intentionally begin to restart a ministry that encompasses some simple joys and pleasures.

In one sense, the ability to be surprised and take risks takes a certain level of humility – admitting that we may not have all the answers. But we can live with contingency and the opposing views of others; we might both be right.

Encourage and celebrate mistakes

Mistakes are a good indicator of mirth and merriment. If people are afraid of getting things wrong, then it tends to suggest a church or vicar who has become 'tight'. The mirth manifesto argues that there is probably an equation or algorithm whereby the lack of mistakes is proportionate to a lack of mirth.

SIGNING UP TO THE MIRTH MANIFESTO 203

The church that signs up to the mirth manifesto might welcome mistakes and celebrate them as a sign of our glorious imperfections and as a victory of effort over skill. Jesus' key disciples were graduates in the school of mistake-making, and Christ saw this as no impediment to high office. The key is not to laugh at the mistakes or the person who made them, but to laugh alongside them, seeing ourselves as fellow error-makers.

I talked to Justin Dodd, a vicar in the Anglo-Catholic tradition. He elegantly captured the beautiful role of mistakes and foibles. The times when a person long-dead suddenly appears on the flower rota is not a case for anger – but can cause a bit of justifiable mirth. At least, that is, if we let it.

> Some of the funniest moments I have had have been at the holiest – the Eucharist. I once cut my head open genuflecting at the altar. At another time I got trapped in my cassock while walking out into the vestry and had to walk backwards into the church, in front of the congregation, to free myself. I think God finds us funny. When we make a mistake, it reminds us that only God doesn't make them.[1]

Mistakes and humility run hand-in-hand, and humility is surely a signal of a church that is growing in mirthfulness. The church that gets too worried about mistakes in the rota, the flowers, or other minor issues, might need to regain some mirth-perspective.

Party without having to add Christian content

Is it just me, or is it annoying that whenever a church puts on a celebration it tends to shoehorn in some godly content? I understand the impulse, especially from the vicar's perspective. You've dragged everyone away from their homes and into church, so let's try to get some messages across.

But the mirth manifesto church simply celebrates whenever it can and celebrates because that in itself is honouring the God who liked to turn water into wine. Local clubs seem to have the edge on us here. When we used to meet for a party at the cricket club I played for, we didn't break off midway to do some batting practise, or have a bowl in the nets. No, we wholeheartedly enjoyed ourselves and laughed and joked and had food and wine. The party was a celebration of all that was good about the club – camaraderie, fun, competition, silliness – and the party helped to bond us as a community and feel a bit better about life.

Mirth might just be an antidote to an overreliance on doctrine and a propensity to perfectionism.

Mirth, and the merriment that often accompanies it, often stands for itself as a testament to the God of good things and happiness.

Do less, run fewer programmes

Sometimes I worry that I am a slacker. But I feel deeply put off by churches that are always doing things – programmes, events and so on. I tend to feel exhausted just thinking about it. I wonder if the mirthful church that loves to be merry might *do* less and *be* more. Might it cut out the odd programme and exchange it for a night at the bowling alley, a trip to the pub or a visit to the seaside? Or simply just provide the space to be with one's family and friends?

Perhaps being mirthful and merry as a way of life and faith is to abandon the need to be certain about everything, to abandon the need to cross every t and dot every i. Would the mirthful church be one where it was OK to be distracted, to finish mid-sentence and know that it is very possible that others have answers just as passionately held and thought-through as our own?

Don't tell people off 'in love'

Mirth and merriment can be tender saplings. It only takes a piece of judgement camouflaged as advice to make someone go into their shell, go elsewhere or feel uncomfortable about being themselves. It's a bit like a worship band playing a pop song as a way of limbering up and being told 'in love' that they shouldn't be playing something written by a person who lived an ungodly life. That would surely end any merriment, right there.

> Mirth and merriment can be tender saplings.

Find people adorable – and funny

How do you react to the foibles and eccentricities of people? The person who tells the same story every time you meet them? The person who turns up very early to church at the precise moment you like to have a quiet and reflective cup of tea? *The Vicar of Dibley* was on the money here, and the Revd Geraldine Granger an object lesson in not just tolerating the human beings God had brought to her but loving their eccentricities and oddness. If God finds people adorable, then the mirthful church must do just the same.

Redraw the lines?

If we want to open up church and life to a richer palette of mirth and humour, might we need to think about redrawing lines? None of us would welcome blasphemy – but what is appropriate, and when? Might we need to leave room for a broader mirth? Is church just too genteel – and judgemental? Take the example of when the *Monty Python* team put out their film *Monty Python's Life of Brian*,[2] back in 1979. Many of us have seen the interview that took place on the late-night show, *Friday Night, Saturday Morning* at the time – featuring an awkward Malcolm Muggeridge and Bishop Mervyn Stockwood and John Cleese and Michael Palin from the Pythons. The representatives of the faith and the church sat po-faced and lambasted the film. The unfortunate host was Tim Rice.

The mirthful and merry church might wonder about whether to take offence *less* often and to give miscreants, the potty mouths and dangerous jokers the benefit of the doubt. We might need to sacrifice some control and safety. We might need to be prepared to laugh until we feel helpless. Laughter is very democratic – anyone can do it, and democracy is a threat to some as well as a blessing to others.

Of course, the essence of the faith is never to gratuitously give offence. But maybe we need to ask whether we should *take* offence so often. If a person says something clumsy but means well, then perhaps we might live with it.

Study questions

The church that signs up to the mirth manifesto might welcome mistakes and celebrate them as a sign of our glorious imperfections and as a victory of effort over skill. Jesus' key disciples were graduates in the school of mistake-making, and Christ saw this as no impediment to high office. The key is not to laugh at the mistakes or the person who made them, but to laugh alongside them, seeing ourselves as fellow error-makers.

How might you sign up to the ministry of mistakes?

Might it cut out the odd programme and exchange it for a night at the bowling alley, a trip to the pub or a visit to the seaside? Or simply just provide the space to be with one's family and friends?

Is this something your church might do? What other non-religious activities can you think of?

If we want to open up church and life to a richer palette of mirth and humour, might we need to think about redrawing lines? None of us would welcome blasphemy – but what is appropriate, and when?

What do you think would be appropriate?

Prayer

Dear Father, thank you for our journey into the heart of mirth and merriment. Help us to be mirthful even when life is tough. Help our churches to be places of joy and hope. Let us not take ourselves too seriously.

Last Word

As I was putting the finishing touches to this book, I met Phil Stone, director of the Scargill Movement,[1] in his office in the beautiful Yorkshire Dales. I know what to expect as the first thing I see is the set of Holy Trinity figures on his desk – made up of three Gruffalo.[2]

He was rooting around in a book and exclaimed that he had found what he'd been looking for. It was a quote from Christian mystic Meister Eckhart on the Trinity which describes how we are born from the laughter of the Trinity. And the laughter between the Father and the Son gives pleasure, which gives joy, which in turn gives love, and that love is the Holy Spirit.[3]

Phil said they took laughter very seriously at the Scargill Movement – a community of Christians from around the world, of various denominations – and that they wanted to include laughter in their Rule of Life. 'Laughter opens people up to God,' Phil said. He encouraged me to put being silly in my mirth manifesto.

He told me that when he ran one of his workshops, he looked at the feedback sheets afterwards. He often received the following: that the teaching was OK but what people really enjoyed was the love and laughter. This is surely something very profound.

Church tends to think it has to be the other way round. 'The teaching was brilliant but the atmosphere wasn't all that.' Perhaps the mirthful church is happy to turn the paradigm on its head. What draws people to God – at least, people living in the twenty-first century – is the atmosphere of joy and fun. Relax; it might be OK to spend a bit less time on the sermon.

Phil reflected – and this was before the Covid-19 pandemic – that the church was at an anxious point in its history. Numbers in the pews were falling. But there was much to smile about. Not least the fact that Christians were, and are, called to be caught up in what God is *already* doing.

> We don't need to fret.

He told me, 'Steve, tell people we don't need to fret.' Maybe that's what's at the heart of mirth. I think it is.

NOTES

[1] Excerpt taken by permission from DECISION Magazine, September 1963, 'An Interview With C.S. Lewis,' by Sherwood E. Wirt. ©1963 Billy Graham Evangelistic Association. All Rights Reserved.

1 First Word

[1] This joke, in various versions, is available very widely on internet joke sites. I do not claim any originality in it. The author of the joke remains a mystery.

2 The Quest Begins

[1] Dalai Lama, Desmond Tutu, *The Book of Joy* (London: Hutchinson, 2016).
[2] Ibid., p. 68.

3   These synonyms have been collected from various internet sources.
4   See P. Frankopan, *The Silk Roads* (London: Bloomsbury, 2015), p. 58.
5   See T. Radcliffe, *Why Go To Church?* (London: Continuum, 2008), p. 1.
6   https://www.thevintagenews.com/2018/08/31/alexamenos-graffito/ (accessed 1 February 2021).

3 The Mirth and Merriment I Grew Up With

1   M. Young and P. Willmott, *Family and Kinship in East London* (London: Penguin Classics, 1957).
2   Released in 2018 (UK: 2019). Distributed by Entertainment One Films.
3   T. Eagleton, *Humour* (New Haven, CT: Yale University Press, 2019), p. 96.

6 Jesus and Humour

1   G.K. Chesterton, *Orthodoxy* (New York: John Lane Co., 1908).

7 The Incarnation

1   J. Cary, *The Sacred Art of Joking* (London: SPCK, 2019).

8 Politics, Fools and Speaking into Power

[1] E.B. White, *Essays of E.B. White* (NY: HarperCollins, 1999), p. 306.

[2] See Ian Frazier, 'Old Hatreds,' in *The New Yorker*, 26 August 2019. https://www.newyorker.com/magazine/2019/08/26/when-w-e-b-du-bois-made-a-laughingstock-of-a-white-supremacist (accessed 2 February 2021).

[3] M. Grant, *The Passing of the Great Race* (New York: C. Scribner's Sons, 1916).

[4] U. Eco, *The Name of the Rose* (New York: Vintage Classics, 2004).

[5] www.learnreligions.com/saint-francis-assisi-sermon-to-birds-124321 (accessed 2 February 2021).

[6] Released in 1986. Distributed by 20th Century Fox.

[7] *Beating Hitler with Humour*, Radio 4, 1 September 2019.

9 Of Golf Courses and Helter-skelters

[1] https://www.dailymail.co.uk/news/article-7095049/Holy-one-Nine-hole-crazy-golf-course-installed-Rochester-Cathedral.html (accessed 2 February 2021).

[2] https://www.bbc.co.uk/news/uk-england-kent-49349348 (accessed 11 February 2021).

[3] https://www.dailymail.co.uk/news/article-7297203/amp/Churchgoers-slam-cathedral-bosses-turn-medieval-nave-nine-hole-CRAZY-GOLF-course.html (accessed 2 February 2021).

[4] https://www.bbc.co.uk/news/av/uk-england-49285829 (accessed 4 February 2021).

[5] Email conversation with the author, 20 August 2019.

10 The Unintentional Merriment and Mirth of Church

[1] Even St Paul suffered from this – see Romans 7:15.
[2] See Philip Yancey, *The Jesus I Never Knew* (Grand Rapids, MI: Zondervan, 1995), pp. 189,190.

11 The Comedy Vicar

[1] F. Butler-Gallie, *A Field Guide to the English Clergy* (London: Oneworld Publications, 2018).
[2] L. Sterne, *The Life and Opinions of Tristram Shandy, Gentleman* (Oxford: OUP, rev. edn, 2009).
[3] See https://www.theguardian.com/film/2005/nov/29/features.johnmullan (accessed August 2019). The article is very good at explaining the vicar and British consciousness.
[4] M.C. Battestin, ed., *Henry Fielding: Joseph Andrews* (Oxford: OUP, 1966).

12 Stand-up and Be Counted

[1] A loop pedal is a piece of technology that records your performance when you tap it. When you tap it again it stops recording and immediately plays back your performance. This allows, for instance, a musician to overdub themselves even while in front of their audience, and they can continue and build up more and more layers of sound.

13 Bring on the Clowns

[1] http://www.holy-fools.org.uk/?page_id=96 (accessed 28 January 2021).

[2] https://www.churchtimes.co.uk/articles/2016/16-september/gazette/obituaries/the-revd-roly-bain (accessed 2 February 2021).

14 Foolish Saint: Martin Luther

[1] https://www.saintlawrencewr.org/about-saint-lawrence-the-martyr.html (accessed 28 January 2021).

[2] See www.lutheranreformation.org/history (accessed 2 February 2021).

[3] See E.W. Gritsch, *The Wit of Martin Luther* (MN: Minneapolis: Fortress Press, 2006), p. 29.

[4] Gritsch, *The Wit of Martin Luther*, p. 5.

15 The Holy Fool: St Francis

[1] G. Birkbeck and N. Hill, eds, *Johnsonian Miscellanies, Volume 2* (NY: Harper & Brothers, 1897).

16 Building the Merry and Mirthful Church

[1] Email to the author on 25 August 2019.

[2] In conversation with the author, November 2019. Edited for use in this book.
[3] E. Trueblood, *The Humor of Christ* (NY: Harper & Row, 1964), p. 32.
[4] See 1 Corinthians 14.
[5] See www.catholic.org/saints/ruleSaintBenedict.php (accessed 11 February 2021).
[6] M. Yaconelli, *Messy Spirituality: Christianity for the Rest of Us* (London: Hodder & Stoughton, 2001).
[7] Nadia Bolz-Weber, *Accidental Saints: Finding God in All the Wrong People* (London: Canterbury Press, 2015).
[8] Dave Tomlinson, *How to Be a Bad Christian* (London: Hodder & Stoughton, 2013).
[9] Interview with the author, February 2019.
[10] See https://www.fourfourtwo.com/features/leeds-united-pantomime-bremner-buttons-hunter-prince-charming (accessed 20 October 2019).

17 Signing Up to the Mirth Manifesto

[1] Interview with author, 19 October 2019.
[2] Released in 1979. Distributed by Cinema International Corporation.

18 Last Word

[1] https://scargillmovement.org/community/ (accessed 29 January 2021).

NOTES

2 A fantasy character from the children's book by Julia Donaldson, *The Gruffalo* (London: Macmillan, 1999).

3 Eckhart von Hochheim, *Meditations with Meister Eckhart* (trans. and ed. Matthew Fox; Bear and Company, 1983), p. 129.